I Hike

I Hike

Mostly True Stories from 10,000 Miles of Hiking

Lawton Grinter

GRAND MESA PRESS

Wheat Ridge, Colorado

Grinter, Lawton.

I hike : mostly true stories from 10,000 miles of hiking / by Lawton Grinter.

Published by: Grand Mesa Press
                  P.O. Box 1854
                  Wheat Ridge, Colorado 80034
                  info@grandmesapress.com

Cover photo courtesy of Richard Larson
Cover design: Lawton Grinter

ISBN 978-0-9852415-0-6 (pbk.)

Library of Congress Control Number: 2012935240
Library of Congress subject headings:
1. Hiking—United States—Biography. 2. Adventure and adventurers—United States—Biography. 3. Appalachian Trail—Description and travel. 4. Pacific Crest Trail—Description and travel. 5. Continental Divide Trail—Description and travel. 6. Grinter, Lawton—1976—Travel. I. Title.

For Jake

~ **Contents** ~

~ Foreword ~

If you bought this book thinking it was some kind of instruction manual for a new Apple product involving Cyber Backpacking, please stop now . . . you've either been sorely misled by some marketing demon and/or you were in the wrong section of the bookstore.

I Hike is a collection of yarns involving walks in the woods, trail towns, long-distance hikers, etc. (this, obviously, for those who didn't read the back cover) by one Lawton "Disco" Grinter (an Author's name if there ever was one). Disco is an inquisitive and trek-mad lad who initially made my acquaintance by constantly pestering me for video editing advice while putting together his fine film about hiking the Continental Divide Trail, *The Walkumentary*. What seemed like every day for WEEKS, I would receive in my inbox questions like, "When you shot your films about the Pacific Crest Trail, which are excellent by the way and I think everyone should own them, they're available at squatchfilms.com, right? Anyway, what was your procedure for interviewing people? Did you walk up to them on the trail with the camera running? (no). Would you entice them with snacks? (sometimes). Were you fully-clothed? (mostly)." Like I said, he's inquisitive. My most persistent rejoinder to his inquiries was to keep the film tight, economical and non-boring. For *The Walkumentary* (his first film), I thought he did a most excellent job. I can also tell you he took that advice towards writing this book.

What is it about trail stories that are cool? I suppose it has a lot to do with the stripped-down nature of being out in the woods for prolonged periods of time. The 9-to-5 BS pretty much evaporates and you actually start to crave social interaction after spending eight hours of walking alone with thoughts spinning around in your head like, "Why am I walking for eight hours alone?" You then run into someone and, for the most part, it's great. The gums start flapping. Food and poop advice flow freely. You really do seem to, seriously, get to know people better in an environment like a long-distance trail. There's actually time to bond.

One of my favorite trail encounters occurred this past year after getting lost on the Appalachian Trail (no easy feat). On my way back down to the trail after finally using the GPS app I had never opened, I ran into one Bob "Buffoon" Siebel who was heading up the side trail I was heading back down following my realization of boneheadedness. He asked me if we were on the AT. I informed him, no. This set off a litany of curse words beautifully resonating through the pines that must have horrified several nearby hikers and some already-nervous squirrels. All this accentuated by his raspy yet joyous 69 year-old Boston-accented voice. It was awesome. When we both arrived near where we should have continued on the AT, I found out he was a still-working stand-up comic. I told him I had done stand-up for 12 years. A look of realized synchronicity washed over his face and he uttered something to the effect of "What are the odds of two stand-ups meeting on a offshoot of the AT?" 236,764 to 1, I told him. He responded that we had to hike together for a while - it was destiny. And so we did. The highlight of which was a stay at a shelter somewhere in Vermont a couple of days later. Bob was there when I arrived and a storm was brewing. I begin interviewing him for my film *Flip Flop Flippin'* and in the middle of some insightful meanderings about materialism and thankfulness a hellacious hail storm descended upon us. While several nearby lightning strikes puckered us up, a kid in his late teens arrived, drenched, telling us two more were coming . . . his mom and younger brother. Shortly after the maelstrom ceased, the mom, *Lion Queen*, and her youngest cub arrived. Her trail name, I surmised, came from the fact that she was carrying an approximately 2ft. x 1ft. stuffed lion on the top of her pack, covered in plastic. Either that or she's a huge Disney fan. She was a big gal, about 300 lbs. After changing into a flannel nightgown she asked if we wouldn't mind hearing some trumpet. All seven of us in the shelter responded, perhaps somewhat surprised and hesitantly, in the affirmative. She then proceeded to play a quite good rendition of "Amazing Grace" on a full-sized brass trumpet. Bob commented that in the last couple of days he had now seen a naked hiker and a trumpet player on the AT and where else would that happen?! Minutes later Lion Queen launched into the "Star Spangled Banner" to which Bob uttered "That's it, I'm gonna re-enlist."

As the duskier sky got darker and all of us in the shelter were now in our sleeping bags, one last time, Lion Queen started again on her chosen instrument. This time it was "Taps." Everyone cracked up. Bob chimed in . . . "I hiked the trail for 17 years and this is the best time I've had in the last four days . . . nudity and trumpets . . . (laughs from the others) . . . I can't wait to get home and tell nobody" (Huge laughs from the others). It was a great and wonderful day on the trail. Hope you enjoy this book.

Scott "Squatch" Herriott
Documentary Filmmaker & Long-Distance Hiker
Squatchfilms.com

~ Author's Introduction ~

I never set out to hike 10,000 miles. It just sort of happened over the course of a decade. Don't get me wrong, you don't walk 10,000 miles without a bit of planning – it's not all just happenstance. But I can tell you for a fact that it was never my original intention.

What I found over those 10,000 miles was always a bit different than what I thought I was looking for. The bulk of those miles were completed over four 2,000+ mile thru-hikes. With each of those hikes I initially set out looking for answers. In the end I ended up with more questions.

My first long hike was an end-to-end hike of the Appalachian Trail. It was mostly a post-college adventure but also a hike I felt compelled to do after a good friend of mine met a tragic end far too early in his short life on the AT in 1997. When I stood on Springer Mountain, the AT's southern terminus in Georgia, that fateful day in March of 1999, I had only a four-day backpacking trip at age 16 as my previous hiking experience. My hike of the AT that summer was plagued with self-doubt and adversity. Through persistence and just plain stubbornness, I stood on Mount Katahdin in Maine five months later. I became one of the small minority of folks that completed the 2,100+ mile length of the Appalachian Trail that year.

I also swore I'd never hike another long trail again. By the time I finished the Appalachian Trail I had lost 30 pounds and a battle with giardiasis had left me completely exhausted. However, it wasn't long before I started reflecting on some of the bigger things that had happened to me during that summer.

I had completed a hike of 2,100 miles, a feat that I had not been certain I would accomplish and a goal that 80% of the hikers that year did not complete.

By the following summer I wanted to relive the memories (at least the good ones), so I hiked the Vermont section of the Appalachian Trail again. Roughly 100 miles in length, the Vermont section was a bit easier than I had remembered it being the previous year.

Two years of graduate school at Virginia Tech followed and what I found missing in those years was time outdoors hiking trails. Classes, being a graduate teaching assistant and writing a 130-page thesis left little time to hit the trail even though my apartment was only 20 miles from the "Dragon's Tooth" section of the AT.

To celebrate getting my Master's degree, I flew out West and hiked the 200+ mile John Muir Trail with a couple of friends. There was more to that hike than just completing the trail itself. The John Muir Trail shares almost the same exact trail tread with the much longer 2,600+ mile Pacific Crest Trail. As much as I told myself I'd never hike another long trail again, I was using the John Muir Trail as a testing ground for a thru-hike of the Pacific Crest Trail. Apparently my gluttony for punishment knew no bounds.

Shortly after completing the John Muir Trail, I got an email out of the blue from a guy I had met on the Appalachian Trail. He told me he was planning to thru-hike the Pacific Crest Trail in 2004 and he asked me if I'd be interested in hiking it with him. My email response to him was two words in length; it simply read, "I'm in." A year later he and I stood at the Mexican border in southern California with our feet pointed north.

I was officially hooked on long-distance hiking. That summer's hike was fantastic and I began rearranging my life around future long hikes. Any thoughts of a career or family were thrown to the wind as I worked various jobs, saving every last penny to fund my next hike.

In 2006 I hiked the 2,800-mile Continental Divide Trail with my girlfriend, a long-distance hiker and reformed engineer named the Princess of Darkness. The Continental Divide Trail put us through the ringer but we persevered and made it to the end with our relationship intact (mostly).

In 2007 I hiked the bulk of the Colorado Trail with a friend I had met on the Pacific Crest Trail in 2004. I spent the following two summers finishing the rest of the Colorado Trail in bits and pieces which my new Colorado zip code allowed me to do fairly easily.

The Princess of Darkness had also completed the Appalachian Trail in addition to the Continental Divide Trail. She also wanted to hike the Pacific Crest Trail partly because it was there and partly because she wanted to become a triple crowner and mostly because it was a better alternative than a summer of working 40 hours a week. I told her that I couldn't let her have all the fun without me so I tagged along and hiked the PCT again. That summer's hike went off like a dream; it was even better than my first PCT thru-hike.

In 2009, we hiked the Tahoe Rim Trail and then decided that it was time to get jobs, get her a Master's degree and buckle down in the work-a-day world for a while. I sometimes found myself at work staring into space, transported to a specific moment on one of my long hikes. There was the time that a complete stranger handed me a $20 bill just because I was hiking, the time that I ate a half-gallon of ice cream in 33 minutes because that is what hikers do when they reach the halfway point of the Appalachian Trail, the time when I thought Princess of Darkness was going to be swept to her death in a roaring river in California and the time when the batteries in my headlamp died as I was hastily trying to get the hell out of a campsite that had just been occupied by 3 black bears. These flashbacks always seemed to cover both the highs and the lows of my time out hiking 10,000 miles with no discrimination as to the good memories or the bad. These flashbacks are the stories I always seem to go to while sharing a campfire with fellow long-distance hikers. These flashbacks are what you are about to read.

I briefly considered writing a book about just one of my long hikes. However, there are dozens of non-fictional narrative accounts out there that chronicle hikers' journeys from the beginning to the end of a single trail. A book of that nature would not allow me to offer anything new to you, the reader. I don't aim to take anything away from that style of book as I've garnered much inspiration and an excess of laughs from those accounts. Bill Bryson's *A Walk in the Woods* is probably the most famous of these first hand accounts (and also one of the funniest).

I opted to take a different approach with this book. The book's contents jump around in place and time over the course of a decade's worth of long-distance hiking on a multitude of the longest trails in the US. It's essentially a "greatest hits" version of things that happened to me on all these trails. Some of those "hits" were truly great. Some were tragic.

Before I let you get to the task at hand, a disclaimer is in order. Edward Abbey wrote in his introduction to *Desert Solitaire* that "All of the persons or places in this book are or were real." That also holds true for the book you now hold in your hands. I changed a few names here and there to protect both the innocent and the guilty. I'm sure they won't mind and I hope you won't either. After all, I subtitled the book "Mostly True Stories from 10,000 Miles of Hiking" to give myself a little breathing room.

I hope my next 10,000 miles proves as fruitful as the first 10,000. If so, perhaps I'll write another book. Enjoy.

Lawton "Disco" Grinter
January 2012
My Brother's Bar
Denver

1

I Hike

"You mean you don't have a car?"

"No," I offered.

"What about a job? You have a job, don't you?"

"No . . . can't have a job when you are walking from Canada to Mexico," I quipped.

The gentleman looked us over, scratched the bald spot on top of his head and glanced at his wife. Then he asked me the one question that is supposed to define our identity and self-worth as people:

"Well, what do you do?" he queried.

"I hike," I said with a grin on my face.

"You hike?" he said skeptically.

"That's right, I hike," I confirmed with the most serious demeanor I could muster.

Our friend paused and then cleared his throat looking over my shoulder at the trail heading off into the spruce trees behind us.

"Well, how long will it take you to do this hike?" he asked.

"About five months total," P.O.D. said with a smile. She's got a lot more patience than I do when it comes to answering the standard questions.

Another scratch of the head. "How'd you get five months off work?"

"We couldn't get five months off so we quit our jobs," I submitted. "They only wanted to give me two weeks vacation and I needed twenty."

"Huh?" our RV-driving friend mumbled, dumbfounded.

Looking back on our conversation with this guy and his wife, I now realize that it actually was very hard for them to fathom who we were, what we were doing and why we needed a ride. We had just walked 700 miles from the Canadian border along the Continental Divide Trail to Yellowstone National Park. We explained this to the both of them and they simply could not comprehend it. The male half of this duo felt certain that we must be using a car or some other type of motorized transportation to propel us along this trail. And how was it possible that we did not have jobs and were taking a five-month vacation? No one in the U.S. gets that kind of time off, right?

It was the summer of 2006 and the Princess of Darkness (P.O.D.) and I were on a thru-hike of the Continental Divide Trail or the "CDT" as it's called in hiker circles. "Thru-hike" meaning we were hiking thru from one end to the other - in the CDT's case, that would be Canada to Mexico via Montana, Idaho, Wyoming, Colorado & New Mexico.

We had been hiking on and off all summer with people named "Skittles," "Lovebarge," "Speedo," "Pi," "Cheech & Chong," "Tradja," "Nacho" and "Pepper." In the long-distance hiking community, most folks choose to abandon their birth names while "on trail" and don a trail name. It is custom for another hiker to give you your trail name . . . usually related to some quirk in your personality or something ridiculous that happens to you while on trail.

I got the trail name "Disco" on my first thru-hike: an end-to-end hike of the Appalachian Trail (AT) from Georgia to Maine in 1999. I started the AT with a high school buddy who happened to see me lose my footing and careen down an unbelievably wet and muddy embankment towards a swollen creek. When I stopped moving I found myself with two feet and one hand planted in the ice cold stream and one hand pointed straight up toward the heavens to keep my balance. My backpack was a mere two inches above the ice-cold current but completely dry. As soon as I realized I wasn't in imminent danger or mangled, I looked over to see my buddy Titus' facial expression . . . a mix of sheer horror and delight as he had witnessed the whole thing from 10 feet away.

"Man, you look like a Disco Inferno! Burn baby burn!!" he exclaimed.

I slowly released the John Travolta pose in which I had landed and gathered myself out of the stream. I made my way back to dry land with water pouring out of my running shoes.

Titus was howling with laughter by this point, yelling "burn baby burn" over and over.

"That's it . . . that's the name . . . Disco Inferno!" I announced to him.

"That's my trail name!"

We hiked on and had a good long laugh about my little mishap. For the sake of brevity, I decided to shorten it and just go with "Disco." Over a decade later, I still go by Disco in certain circles - both on and off the trail.

Disco is a relatively benign trail name compared to some others that I've heard: Flem, Snotrocket, Scrote, Vulture Death and Vagisil. Yes Vagisil. Apparently they called him "Vadge" for short. And yes it was a he. Vadge got his unfortunate trail name because he kept a tube of Vagisil in his first aid kit to treat chafing – a skin irritation that occurs when both legs rub together over the course of many miles of hiking. He swears the product Vagisil is officially recommended to treat chafing in a popular hiking guidebook. The best part is that Vadge is a 6'4"

Brit with a thick accent and would proudly tell perfect strangers his trail name when asked.

P.O.D. got the trail name "Princess of Darkness" from her mischievous nature. She had originally been given the trail name "Boats" due to some oversized camp shoes she had been wearing in the evenings on the AT but that name didn't stick. One too many pranks and a little too much taunting of her fellow hikers led to her being renamed the "Princess of Darkness" on her AT thru-hike in 2002.

She recently suggested to me that we use trail names during our wedding ceremony. I don't think this would be legal in most states and I doubt our families would find it as relevant as we might. We have logged over 5,000 miles of hiking together in the last three years and have spent much of that time calling each other P.O.D. and Disco. Perhaps I should query our county's Justice of the Peace to see what he thinks of marrying a couple named the Princess of Darkness and Disco.

***

P.O.D. and I were trying to "yogi" a ride from the balding owner of the RV and his wife to Grants Campground eight miles down the road in Yellowstone National Park. Our odds of getting a ride from them would greatly increase if he actually believed that we were walking from Canada to Mexico. "Yogi-ing" is a fine art and most all hikers do it to some degree or another during a long-distance hike. In its simplest form, it is a method used to get a person to give you or offer you something that you need without asking for it directly. This guy was going to be a hard sell.

P.O.D. has mastered the technique with a lot more sophistication than I could ever hope to. A week or so after we left Yellowstone, we found ourselves traversing the Wind River

Range, a string of craggy mountains in central Wyoming, and running low on food due to poor planning and a reluctance to carry heavy packs. When your body is burning 4,000 – 6,000 calories per day, it's hard to pack enough food to compensate. Doing so would require carrying a backpack the size of a VW Bug and weighing nearly as much. We had already started rationing the little food we had left that week. There is nothing worse than eating only half a granola bar when your appetite would allow you to easily devour a small truckload of granola bars.

It was a summer weekend in the "Winds," which meant the masses would be bagging peaks and sweating out the workweek . . . and lots of them were headed into the Winds as we were headed out.

"Do you know how far it is to Big Sandy Lodge?" P.O.D. asked the couple getting ready to hike right past us.

"It's about 15 or 16 miles. We just came from there," the polite guy with the brand new backpack told us.

"Do you know if they sell food?" P.O.D. quickly asked.

I was wondering what the heck P.O.D. was doing. We had just sat down 30 minutes prior to running into this couple, looked at a map and knew that we were exactly 16 miles from Big Sandy Lodge. We also knew they offered a big family style dinner nightly if they weren't full of guests.

"They do. They have an all-you-can-eat dinner if you get there by six."

"That's a relief to hear. We are almost out of food and could devour an all-you-can-eat dinner. We're hiking the CDT from Canada to Mexico and have been hiking for two months now and we are starving," P.O.D. stated promptly.

"You're hiking the entire trail?" the guy shockingly asked.

"Yes and we need to get to that lodge quick to get some food!"

"Well it's 16 miles and you're not going to make it today. My wife and I are carrying way too much food for two nights. Can we give you some?" the man asked.

P.O.D. replied, "Oh gosh, we'd hate to take your food."

"We insist. We have way too much and my pack is killing my shoulders," the lady replied.

At this point, the couple heaved their packs onto the ground with a grunt. They dug down to find their food bags, which resembled 60-gallon drums and appeared to weigh more than a full-grown Great Dane. Granola bars, trail mix, pistachios, tuna (all hikers carry tuna for some ungodly reason), almonds and peanut butter. They pulled the items out one by one and plunked them on the ground beside their packs.

We thanked them profusely and proceeded to eat most everything they gave us on the spot. It was wonderful. I almost felt full enough to hike another hour before being hungry again.

Once we got out of earshot of the couple I told P.O.D. that she deserved an Oscar for her acting performance.

"That wasn't acting. I was starving!!!" she offered to me in all sincerity.

"Hey, is that another couple up ahead?" she asked with an earnest voice as I glanced down the trail to see two more hikers ambling towards us.

***

We hadn't planned on going to any of the big car campgrounds while in Yellowstone including the one we were trying to get a ride to now. There was no need as we were without a car and weren't interested in paying $15 to camp when we could camp along the CDT for free. However, I miscalculated the amount of time we'd be hiking through the park and now we needed a ride to Grants Campground to get the proper permit to camp in Yellowstone at night in "the backcountry."

National Parks divide the land inside their park boundaries into two separate categories: the "frontcountry" and the "backcountry." The frontcountry consists of visitor centers, roads, sidewalks, vending machines, hotels (yes some National Parks have hotels), and anything else that is paved or contains a roof. If you walk 30 feet or more from anything paved and are not in an enclosed building, you've entered the backcountry. Walk 30 feet off Skyline Drive in Shenandoah National Park in Virginia along the Appalachian Trail and you will encounter signs telling you that you have entered the backcountry. For some reason, I always find it comical that I need a sign to let me know I'm out in the woods.

National Parks present unique problems to long-distance hikers almost solely because we do not arrive at a park in a vehicle as 99% of park visitors do. We arrive on foot. In the case of Yellowstone, those of us going southbound on the CDT arrive on foot on the far southwest side of the Park in the middle of nowhere. There is no one at that park boundary to charge us money, give us a brochure and move us through a gate. There is no gate; just a sign letting you know you've entered the park and a second sign letting you know what you are not allowed to do in the park. You are not allowed to have guns, pets or camp without a permit.

Camping without a permit will land you a $200 fine (if caught). Backcountry camping permits at Yellowstone are available at a few specific ranger stations within the park. 99% of folks either mail in an advance registration form to request a campsite or they show up in person to get a permit by driving to a ranger station most readily accessible by car.

On a thru-hike there is no possible way to know in advance what nights you will be camping at a specific location in a park especially when it takes six weeks just to hike to the park from the Canadian border. Heck, we rarely knew where we were going to camp hours before doing so on any given day. Our typical modus operandi was to find the first flat spot off the side of the trail once it got dark and call it good.

Most thru-hikers call the permit office from the town of Mack's Inn, Idaho, which is roughly 3-4 days away from Yellowstone on foot, and explain they are thru-hiking the CDT and will be coming through the park in 3-4 days. And most thru-hikers are given special permission to camp in the park without an official backcountry permit tag in hand for the 1st night. Thru-hikers are told to stop by the permit office at Old Faithful Ranger Station to get an official permit once in the park. Making these types of special arrangements with thru-hikers irks the National Park Service to no end.

***

We stopped at the Old Faithful Ranger Station and spent 20 minutes conferring with a friendly ranger and gaining approval for the campsite where we wanted to stay that night. We were told that in Yellowstone, hikers must overnight camp in designated campsites and be in possession of a backcountry camping permit for that specific designated campsite no matter where they are in the entire 2.2 million acre park. We secured a permit for a campsite about seven miles distant and were on our way.

It was getting late in the afternoon and a brief thunderstorm rolled in. Yellowstone has an abundance of geothermal activity and hiking through some of the steaming hot spots made for an eerie scene straight out of *Tales from the Crypt*. Dusk quickly moved to darkness and almost immediately we arrived at an odd trail junction. A quick consultation of our map conveyed that there wasn't supposed to be any trail junction at the spot where we now stood. Hmm. We were carrying a GPS unit which told us our exact location and that we needed to continue southeast to stay on trail. It also told us we were about a mile from our designated campsite (the one we had a permit for).

After a bit of scampering around we found the right trail and headed off. About 20 minutes later, we turned the GPS on to find out how close we were to our campsite. Oddly enough, the GPS showed us standing right on top of it. That was strange because as we looked around our immediate surroundings, there was nothing but trees and waist-high grass. We walked on for another ten minutes. No campsite. Hmm. Now our GPS was showing that we had passed the campsite. It was 10:00 P.M. and we were both beat. We couldn't find our designated campsite and all we wanted to do was set up our tent, crawl in and go to sleep. I had visions of a park ranger finding us in the middle of the night, giving us tickets and making us leave the park. P.O.D. told me that I was being ridiculous.

"No park ranger in their right mind would be walking around out here at ten o'clock at night," she proclaimed.

After a bit of debate, we decided that we would head off into some nearby pines out of view from the trail. If by chance a park ranger out for a stroll in the middle of the night happened upon us, we would plead our case and proclaim that we had to make an "emergency" camp because we could not find the designated campsite. If by chance one of the 300 grizzly bears that inhabit Yellowstone National Park happened upon us in the middle of the night, no one might ever find us. I'd prefer a park ranger over a grizzly.

The night went off without a hitch and we were left unmolested by bears and park rangers. We got an early start though, just to lessen our chances of being fined for illegally camping on public land.

At our first snack break of the day I realized that I had made another miscalculation. I thought we had 22 more miles left to get out of the park and as it turned out, we had 32. It wasn't out of the realm of possibility to hike 32 miles in a day, but doing so just to get outside of the park boundary seemed absurd. We would once again need to get another backcountry permit to camp in the backcountry in Yellowstone National Park. Our map showed the trail crossing a road in a couple of miles. That road headed eight short miles into Grants Campground, which had a backcountry permit station. If we wanted to be legal, we needed to get a ride to that permit station.

Oh, and the other thing - it is illegal to hitchhike anywhere within national parks. So technically we could not put our thumb out to get a ride to the permit station, which brings us back to our couple - the ones in disbelief that we just walked 700 miles from Canada to that very spot where the CDT crossed the road heading to Grants Campground. The ones that we needed to drive us to Grants Campground. Our initial attempts at yogi-ing a ride from them had failed. We just wanted to get our stupid permit. It was time to pull out all the stops.

"We really need to get a permit and would love a ride to the permit station if you are headed towards Grants Campground," P.O.D. said with a hint of desperation.

"Nah, nope, not headed that way, headed the other way," the man said not giving much consideration to our plight.

"So how do you get your jobs back once your done hiking?" he immediately asked, still bewildered by what we were doing.

"You know, the park service should really kill all the wolves in the park. They hunt for sport," the wife added.

At this point in the conversation, both P.O.D. and I knew that we needed to hit the eject button. It was obvious that these folks were not going to give us a ride to the permit station and that any discussion with this lady about shooting wolves in national parks would probably lead to hurt feelings and my saying something I probably shouldn't have.

"So where do you take showers? Do they have showers set up along the trail?" the guy asked next.

"We've got to be going," I announced. "You all have a nice day."

With that we walked over to the side of the road and stuck out our thumbs. We were picked up within five minutes by a nice family from Colorado on summer vacation. They took us straight to the permit station and didn't mention shooting wolves, jobs or where our car was.

2

Ice Cream Headache

Pine Grove Furnace State Park is a modest 700-acre parcel of woodlands in central Pennsylvania that pays tribute to the iron smelting that occurred there as early as the 1700's. It is also the halfway point between Georgia and Maine for Appalachian Trail thru-hikers. The convenience store on its premises sells half-gallons of ice cream. What better way to celebrate having just walked over 1,000 miles than by slurping down four pints of ice cream in under one hour?! The vast majority of AT hikers that reach Pine Grove Furnace State Park attempt to do just that.

There had been talk on trail for weeks about the "Half-Gallon Challenge" leading up to our arriving at Pine Grove Furnace. Most every hiker I ran into was going to give it a shot with only a small handful relenting.

Everyone had his or her own strategy: from what flavor they would choose, to whether or not they would fast before their attempt, mental preparation techniques and on who had the best odds of completing the challenge.

"Ox has got it in the bag. I saw him eat three combo meals at McDonalds in Waynesboro and then hike 16 miles without breaking a sweat," one hiker told me.

"Have you seen "Big Girl" eat? Holy cow! He could put down a half-gallon of ice cream and then go have breakfast," another hiker piped in.

I'd been hiking with a guy named "Ice House" for a few days who told me that every few hours he would do mental visualizations of successfully scarfing down the half-gallon with ease and plenty of time to spare before his hour was up. He said that if he could mentally convince himself it was possible, he'd have no trouble completing this mission once he got to Pine Grove Furnace.

I had my own personal doubts about whether or not I could do it. However, I figured I should take a crack at it or else face the severe chiding from my fellow hikers that would inevitably occur if I shied away. All I knew is that the most ice cream I had ever eaten in one sitting while on trail or anywhere else for that matter was a single pint of Ben & Jerry's. Now I was going to try and eat four times that amount – in 60 minutes.

***

Food challenges are not uncommon on long trails. The AT's Half-Gallon Challenge had been going on for decades by the time I showed up in person at Pine Grove Furnace in 1999 to give it a go.

The Pacific Crest Trail (PCT) has it's own food challenge – the "Pancake Challenge" in the northern California settlement of Seiad Valley. The Seiad Cafe's pancake challenge gained such notoriety that it was featured on the Travel Channel's "Top 10 Places to Pig Out." The flapjacks are so big that the cook uses a large metal dustpan to flip them, which makes sense considering they weigh in at a pound apiece. To complete the challenge you have to eat five of these colossal cakes in two hours . . . and keep it down.

Many PCT hikers have attempted this challenge and most all of them have failed. Some failed miserably like "So Far" in 2003 who ate his first three pancakes in 20 minutes. A couple of bites into his fourth pancake, he proceeded to upchuck every last piece of dough he had just ingested in front of a crowd of gawking onlookers that included both his mom and former scoutmaster. He later told me, "It was a very controlled little squirt, much like soft-serve ice cream being poured into a little dish. It looked exactly like oatmeal and had my mother not immediately objected, the plan was to eat it again and carry on with the challenge. After all, if you ate it, it was free."

The other aspect of the PCT's pancake challenge that makes it less than appealing is that hiker's are faced with a stiff 4,000' climb over the next six miles as they head north out of town on the trail. So imagine for a moment that you have just stuffed 80 ounces of doughy pancakes into your belly, put on a fully loaded pack, and then hiked uphill 4,000' in the humidity-infused heat of the northern California summer while incessantly swatting at the 200 gnats that are dive bombing your eyes. Boot camp sounds preferable, doesn't it?

In 2000, some AT hikers, apparently emboldened by their success in the Half-Gallon Challenge, mounted an attempt at a 20,000-calorie challenge in Gorham, New Hampshire to celebrate hiking in the millennium year. I guess the 5,000 calories ingested in their successful half-gallon challenges were just not enough for this sordid few.

Consider here that the recommended daily allowance of calories for the average US adult is 2,000; these hikers were now going to try and eat 10 times that amount. To put this in perspective, you would need to eat 37 McDonald's Big Macs to accomplish this feat. 37. I would recommend having an ambulance on stand by or a colonic appointment set up in advance at a minimum.

Needless to say, they didn't make it that far. Some were able to get 10,000 calories down before tapping out. Others regurgitated. Some had to take a "zero day" (a day of no hiking) just to recover, while others swore that they would never consider trying anything that dumb ever again.

In 2006, a German hiker on the PCT named "Heike" told everyone she could easily drink a gallon of milk in one sitting. "I am German. I have been drinking milk my whole life. This will be no problem," she boasted in a thick Deutschlandic accent to the crowd of hikers gathered around at the Saufleys. The Saufleys are a couple who live in the small outpost of Agua Dulce on the edge of the southern California desert and allow PCT thru-hikers to camp in their back yard. Most hikers reach the Saufleys about a month after they start their treks from the Mexican border. Because the bulk of hikers start their thru-hikes at the same time on the last weekend of April, it is not uncommon for 50 or more hikers to bottleneck at the Saufleys in late May. The day Heike attempted her milk challenge, there were roughly 40+ hikers in attendance and all sat in awe at the spectacle before them.

I wasn't present but I did see the video footage as has anyone who has watched *Even More Walking*, a documentary about PCT thru-hikers by Scott "Squatch" Herriot. She had consumed 124 of the 128 ounces she needed to get the entire gallon down in under an hour. With four ounces to go she stood up - her pupils dilated - and she lurched forward, proceeding to projectile vomit a fountain of white milk with the force of an unabated fire hose. It was not pretty and she lost the $200 bet.

What strange phenomenon spurs long-distance hikers to attempt such food challenges? Is it the long hot dusty days spent eating "tuna-mac" and ramen noodles that leave hikers fantasizing about restaurant food? Is it the ravenous appetites most hikers possess as a result of burning 6,000 calories per day? Or is it the peer pressure and mob rule that take over when you get a dozen rowdy hikers in one place who have just walked a thousand miles and most of whom are feeling invincible.

I'm not sure, but I never questioned not doing the half-gallon challenge myself. It did not even cross my mind that I could opt for a cheeseburger and fries in lieu of 64 ounces of low quality ice cream. Groupthink had taken over and it was now my destiny to undertake this challenge.

***

June 10, 1999 dawned overcast and chilly. A constant mist greeted Ice House, Wood Doctor and I at the Birch Run shelters some ten miles shy of Pine Grove Furnace State Park. All three of us were going to try the challenge and it was the first thing on everybody's mind that morning as we broke camp.

"Disco, you better start doing those stomach exercises I told you about or you're never gonna get that half-gallon down," Ice House stated emphatically as he hiked out early to get a jump start on the trek to the state park.

"Thankfully the weather gods gave us a warm sunny day to eat four pints of ice cream," I chimed back sarcastically as I glanced at the thermometer on my watch . . . 46 degrees.

We ran into six other hikers on our hike to the store and the chatter went back and forth all day as we planned our final strategies for the challenge. Every one of us was going to try it; no one had chickened out.

"I'm going with straight chocolate . . . no crazy flavored bull-shit," Old Blue told us.

"I'm not going to eat anything until I get there. I should be starving by then and I'll get that half-gallon down in no time flat," Bee strategized.

I spent the first thirty minutes of the hike that morning walking as swiftly as possible just to stay warm. The cold mist and light breeze were raw and the thought of eating ice cream was far from my mind. By mid morning it had warmed up slightly and I was doing the mental visualizations Ice House had recommended. My mind's eye saw still frames of me whipping down a half-gallon of vanilla ice cream with my titanium spork . . . a smile on my face and my spork raised high in the air after my successful completion. These images played over and over in my mind like a movie reel on repeat.

I also used "positive self talk" which psychologists recommend for overcoming a mental or physical obstacle. The idea here is that if you say something to yourself over and over and over, eventually you can convince your mind that it is true, regardless of it's legitimacy. I used this technique twice last summer to get across the finish line of a marathon and half-marathon and can vouch for its success.

"I am strong. I love to run. I feel great."

This subtle little mantra can do wonders when you are at mile 24 of a marathon with 2+ miles to go and every part of your body hurts, running another inch seems next to impossible and collapsing in a heap would be quite preferable.

By the time most of us got to the state park store, a few hikers had arrived early and already finished up their half-gallons. Ice House ate a half-gallon of chocolate in 16 minutes. Never mind that Ice House was built like an NFL fullback.

Even a few of the leaner hikers had pulled it off with time to spare. This gave me hope. One hiker in particular, Peregrine, had finished his half-gallon successfully but looked rather pale. He would go into the bathroom at 15-minute intervals and come out clutching his stomach with somewhat of an exasperated look on his face.

I walked into the store and headed over to the ice cream freezer. I peered through the display glass at an assortment of flavors. Cherries jubilee, banana split, chocolate marshmallow, green mint chip, strawberry cheesecake, vanilla, chocolate and something called heavenly hash. I purchased a half-gallon of vanilla. I wanted the least flagrant flavor possible. And I absolutely did not want to eat a half-gallon of anything with the names "hash" or "cheesecake" in them.

Ice House recommended popping the brick hard half-gallon into the microwave for 20 seconds to soften the sides. I think most store clerks would find this practice odd, but the clerk at the Pine Grove Furnace store didn't even bat an eyelash when I placed my box of vanilla in their microwave. After following Ice House's advice once again, I flipped open the cover of my half gallon to find the inside edges slightly soft like mashed potatoes.

I headed up to the counter to pay for my ice cream.

"You know that you get a wooden spoon if you can finish your ice cream in under one hour," the clerk informed me.

He held up a tiny wooden spoon of the type you would be given to sample a nice sorbet or gelato at a high-end ice cream parlor. On the spoon were the words "1/2 Gallon Club."

So for the first time I fully understood the situation. I had just paid someone five dollars for an ungodly amount of cheap ice cream that I was going to try and devour in less than one hour. If I was able to accomplish this feat without soiling my pants, I would be presented with a tiny wooden spoon for my efforts and become part of an obscure club that no one outside of Pine Grove Furnace State Park or the thru-hiking community would have ever heard of or care about. Sounds brilliant. Bon Appétit!

I walked outside to the metal picnic table on the store's covered porch and plopped down with my half-gallon and titanium spork. I felt nervous and excited at the same time . . . the same exact way I feel every Wednesday night when I check my lottery numbers. I was given some last minute advice from a number of hikers who were already digging in.

"Work your way around the edges. It's soft there and by the time you get to the middle it will have had time to thaw out."

With that last bit of guidance and a few Hail Mary's, I gave one last glance at my watch. 10:25 A.M. I hoisted my spork and started in. My goal was to pace myself a bit and not overdo it in the early stages of the challenge. I knew the last quarter of my ice cream block would be the toughest.

I started working my way around the edges, which were already soft from the microwaving. I made small talk with everyone at the table to stay slightly distracted from the absurdity of what I was doing. Ten minutes had passed and I was already a third of the way done when a hiker named "Rocket" bolted up from the table and ran into the bathroom with a look of sheer panic on his face. He was almost finished with a half-gallon of something called "purple passion." After 15 minutes, he came out of the bathroom and flopped down on the cement.

Incoherently he mumbled something that sounded like, "I'm done."

A few hikers tried to pump him up and get him back at the table but he just rolled around on the cement groaning while clutching his mid-section. He appeared to be in sheer agony. I moved to a different chair so that I would no longer be in direct view of him. I didn't need him psyching me out or putting negative thoughts in my head! I knew I had to focus on the task at hand. I was able to mostly block out his groans but could have benefitted from a pair of earplugs.

Halfway through my ice cream I paused to take stock of how I was feeling. It had only been 15 minutes since I started and I had already consumed 32 ounces of vanilla. Pulse rate seemed to be ok and my stomach showed no signs of distress. I was feeling good and with 45 minutes to spare, my confidence grew at finishing this challenge under the one-hour allotment.

I kept a steady pace as I charged forward boldly through the backside of my half-gallon. I was in the zone, not unlike Tony Hawk when he landed the "900" for the first time or Michael Phelps when he broke multiple world records and finished with eight gold medals in the 2008 Summer Olympics. The more I ate, the more confident I was that I could finish.

I was getting close to the end of my ice cream. All that was left was something resembling an off-white snowball in the middle of my ice cream carton. I kept working off the edges and with one last mouthful, I finished my vanilla and completed the Appalachian Trail's Half-Gallon Challenge. My watch read 10:58 A.M. It took me exactly 33 minutes flat to consume the beast. A quick glance at the nutritional info followed by some simple math told me that I had just downed 32 full servings of ice cream totaling 5,440 calories and 320 grams of fat in a half hour. I shuddered a bit . . . perhaps it was the brain freeze.

I stood up and walked around just to see if I could. Oddly enough, I felt somewhat decent . . . actually quite well. A feeling of pride came over me as I reflected upon my accomplishment. I headed back into the store to obtain my hard-earned award.

"I finished it in 33 minutes," holding the empty carton upside down for the store clerk to see.

"Congratulations," he proclaimed as he pulled a wooden spoon from behind the counter.

"We also sell toilet paper if you need to stock up," he chuckled.

I thanked him for the wooden spoon and told him I might be back in later for toilet paper. I went outside and posed for some celebratory photos with my spoon before gathering my gear and packing up. A number of folks were talking about hiking another seven miles to the Tagg Run shelters before calling it a day. It was noon by now and although I had been waiting for my stomach to revolt, it still felt fine. Hmm. Could I somehow be immune to the pain and anguish most people would experience after gorging 5,400 calories of ice cream in a half hour? Maybe I was. After all, I had just walked over 1,000 miles to get to Pine Grove Furnace and was feeling pretty bullet-proof in general.

Before hiking out I headed into the bathroom to "borrow" a bit of extra toilet paper. It's not uncommon for thru-hikers to sponge a bit of TP from a roll in a public restroom . . . just enough to make it a few days until you hit the next public restroom. I was no exception; I grabbed enough for two to three days and called it good.

I headed out behind everyone that had been at Pine Grove Furnace that day. It had started to mist again and was still a bit chilly, so I was in no hurry to leave the protection of the covered porch at the state park store. I was homeless after all.

It was mid-afternoon by the time I shouldered my backpack and started moving forward. Fairly quickly I passed a hand-made monument that proclaimed "Springer Mountain 1,069 miles South, Katahdin 1,069 miles North." I high-fived the monument and hiked on with a grin on my face. I had just crossed the AT's halfway point and successfully completed the Half-Gallon Challenge all in the same day. Anything was possible now . . . law school, medical school . . . perhaps I should get my pilot's license.

A mile or so later as I was ambling gleefully down the trail, I felt a slight twinge in my stomach. It was not a large twinge but definitely a contraction of some kind. For the next 20 minutes my stomach started making odd noises similar to those creeky coffin door sounds common to Halloween spook houses. I tried to convince myself that I was probably okay and that if the ice cream were to have affected me, it would have done so about an hour ago.

My friend "Buddha" likes to say that when hikers have to go, they usually have to go IMMEDIATELY. Usually it's not even a 10-second countdown. It's more like 10-9-8-2-1-Boom! Explosive diarrhea or "Number 3," as Josh Richman and Anish Sheth refer to it in their book, *What's Your Poo Telling You?*, is an unfortunate experience. It is especially so when you are on trail with nary a flush toilet in a 10-mile radius.

Well, I had less than half the allotted time than what Buddha had suggested. I literally had about one second to look up the trail and back down the trail to make sure no one was around. I took a frantic step and a half off the trail and dropped my shorts.

Typically hikers take the time to walk well off the trail, dig a "cat-hole" 6-8 inches deep, take care of business and then cover the hole back up with dirt and walk away. I didn't have time for any of that. I barely had time to pull my shorts down.

It was over in about 2.5 seconds. The thing about the violent eruption that comprises going #3, is the acute sense of relief that comes immediately following the event. As quickly as it had come, it had gone and I felt fine and new again. I hastily dug my cat hole and gingerly scooped in my offering and spent toilet paper with a couple of sticks lying nearby. I filled in the dirt and was on my way. No harm no foul.

Perhaps it was just an isolated event, I told myself. A one time revolt. A fluke. After all, I surmised that my stomach had to do something in return for ingesting a half-gallon of ice cream. I was fine now and ready to hike onward.

10-9-8-2-1 . . . "Oh no!" I exclaimed as I ran off the trail again, barely able to make it behind a bush before the next round began. It had the force of a class five river rapid. I dug my hole again post-movement and buried the evidence. This was not good. This was not good at all! What was I going to do if this kept up? I only had enough toilet paper to last for a few days and that was based on one to two bathroom breaks per day - not 500. And it's not like I could run down to Wal-Mart to stock up either; I was in the middle of the Pennsylvania woods.

I didn't feel that well, honestly. My stomach took on general distress pains and I was moving slowly. My energy levels had bottomed out. Also, my sweat had taken on an odd aroma . . . something akin to a light vanilla scent. It was coming out of my pores!

Thirty minutes passed without incident. Perhaps I was out of the woods so to speak. I just needed to sweat it out, I told myself. The worst was over. I walked on for another fifteen minutes and out of nowhere, a sizeable stomach contraction hit me with the force of a quarterback sack. "Oh God," I pleaded as I ran off the side of the trail and out of sight of any hikers that might saunter by.

This time I did something completely different that I will never do again. The hiking shorts I was wearing had one of those built in mesh liners, kind of like men's swim trunks. As I was squatting, I placed my ½ roll of TP in the mesh liner for easy access. Normally I place the TP on the ground and tear off what I need while I'm finishing the paper work. I thought it would be more efficient to have the TP a bit closer to me for some reason so I put it in the liner. Well . . . the TP fell into the hole I had dug. That hole contained a large quantity of #3. This was about as bad a situation as I could have possibly imagined.

What was I going to do now? I was barely a half-day out of Pine Grove Furnace state park and had about two full days of hiking to get to the town of Boiling Springs where I could pick up more TP. Backtracking was out of the question. It would have been just too demoralizing to backtrack, especially over something as small as toilet paper. But I was in dire straits. At the rate I was going, I'd probably end up digging about 375 cat holes between now and Boiling Springs and I was going to need TP to make the situation tolerable. More importantly, I was squatting in the bushes at that very moment and in desperate need of something - anything to finish up. I briefly eyed my right sock and thought about using it for my needs, but decided the sock was too valuable serving its current purpose. I couldn't sacrifice the sock. I just couldn't. I looked around to see if anything else was available. It was the middle of summer after all and there were green leaves as far as the eye could see. And a few smooth rocks lying about.

I started with the rocks and finished with the leaves and they more or less did the job. I ended up burying my saturated half roll of TP with the rest of the pile. I hiked on in hopes of finding more TP at the shelter ahead, pulling over at regular 30-45 minute intervals to expel the demons. If the shelter privy had none, I'd beg and plead for some from my fellow hikers. Luckily for me there was an abundance of smooth rocks and green leaves during the rest of my hike into the shelter.

I arrived at the shelter to find Wood Doctor, Honolulu and a few other hikers setting up camp for the night.

"Hey man, you don't look so good. Are you alright?" Wood Doctor asked me. Apparently I was three shades of green.

"The ice cream. Too much," I garbled in reply. It made me think of Peregrine.

I dropped my pack on the shelter's floor and headed immediately over to the privy located on the edge of the woods. I had high hopes of finding a lovely new roll of fluffy white TP in the privy. Actually I had visions of there being an entire case of fluffy white triple ply toilet paper and an immaculate toilet area complete with a cushioned toilet seat and bidet awaiting my arrival. I opened the creaky door of the privy and peered in. A few spiders ran down the hole and cobwebs filled the ceiling of this outhouse. No TP anywhere to be found. Only a tattered brochure proclaiming the need for me to accept Jesus Christ as my lord and savior. The wind had just been taken out of my sails.

I walked back to the shelter to find Wood Doctor setting up his bed for the evening.

"Hey man. I need to ask a favor," I stymied.

"What's up?" he replied.

"I need TP. My stomach revolted all the way from the state park to here and I used up all the TP I had packed out," I confessed with a tone of despair. Never mind the part about my TP falling into my own shit and me having to bury it. I figured he could do without the details.

"You're in luck. My aunt sent me extra TP in my maildrop. I packed out two rolls and you can have one of them. I don't need to be carrying around two rolls anyway . . . too much weight."

I couldn't believe it. It's as if God himself had sent an angel down from heaven. The angel was a bearded hiker named Wood Doctor and he bore the gift of TP. It was a modern day miracle!

Wood Doctor handed me a brand new roll of bright white TP. I didn't even care that it was 1-ply. I held the roll in my hands and gazed at it as if I had been handed the keys to a new car. Wood Doc had just saved my butt.

"I've got Imodium and Pepto-Bismol too. You want some?" he offered.

Imodium is an anti-diarrhea pill that keeps #3 at bay. The motto on the box he handed me said, "So you can quickly get back to doing the things you love." I grabbed a couple Imodiums and some pink Pepto-Bismol pills and consumed the whole lot of them on the spot. I held my new roll of TP tight in my hand and thanked the Wood Doctor profusely.

From this point forward, the sight of ice cream was enough to make me nauseous and I avoided the frozen section of grocery stores for the rest of the trip. I'm convinced to this day that the half-gallon challenge triggered some type of late onset lactose intolerance in my body. I've had trouble with dairy ever since.

If you ever find yourself at Pine Grove Furnace State Park in the ice cream section of the store, do yourself a favor and just buy a pint. And by all means, pack out extra toilet paper.

3

Close Encounters With Hypothermia

The "Great Flood of 2004" started inconspicuously. We paid little attention to the clouds that had been building all day as we made our way towards Rockpile Lake in a remote corner of Oregon's Deschutes National Forest along the Pacific Crest Trail. A grand total of two hours of rain had fallen in the last four months and to say that everyone had become complacent about bad weather and bad weather backpacking gear was a gross understatement.

I had been hiking with "Honolulu" since the Mexican Border and "Trim" off and on since northern California. The three of us set up camp on the far shore of Rockpile Lake in some lofty pines after cooking our trail dinners and enjoying a dessert of Reese's Cups. The clouds over the lake, which had slowly been darkening all day, were now ominous and foreboding. All appearances said that it was now only a matter of an hour, or possibly minutes, until a full-bore tempest released its fury on us.

I walked around my tent and restaked all my guy lines to make sure I had the tautest pitch possible. By the time I was done re-tensioning all the lines, you could have bounced a baby off the side of it. I added rocks over the tops of all the stakes trying to imagine the worst that could happen . . . my tent blowing away with me in it like the balloon boy. I tried to envision how running water would flow under my tent. The last thing I wanted was a soaked down sleeping bag.

Most of the ground on the far side of the lake was relatively bare due to the excessive amount of campers this shoreline campsite had obviously hosted. In a last minute decision that I would be thankful for later, I pulled my groundsheet from under the tent's floor and placed it inside the tent on top of the floor. I realize this defeats the purpose of what a groundsheet is supposed to do, which is rest on the ground between the dirt and the tent's nylon floor to keep twigs and thorns and other debris from poking holes through the nylon. It seemed to me though that water would likely funnel right to the front of my tent and wedge itself between the ground sheet and the tent floor as it made its way down to Honolulu and Trim's shelters. Maybe this was not a big deal for me considering I was camped on a gentle slope and the water would definitely continue downhill, but it was a risk I wasn't willing to take given the ink black color of the clouds that were looming overhead.

Both Trim and Honolulu had camped further down the slope in a low-lying area. Honolulu was under a tarp and Trim had a self-enclosed tent similar to mine. We were basically just waiting and at midnight it began.

Imagine the sound of an afternoon thunderstorm or the repetitious clamor of pouring rain on a metal-roofed house. Typically heavy rains don't last long - maybe thirty minutes or an hour, two hours at the most. Downpours are short-lived events: saturated clouds release a build-up of moisture and then it's over. At least that's how it is supposed to happen. For eight solid hours, we were stuck in our tents imprisoned by a torrential downpour. It poured unendingly from midnight to 8:00 A.M. It did not let up . . . not even once. We were all a bit dismayed to say the least.

This eight-hour deluge was the first of several unseasonably cold storms funneling in off the Pacific that would plague us for four solid weeks until we reached northern Washington on the PCT. Most of Oregon obtained a month's worth of rain in a few days from this storm. Some weather stations reported three times the average monthly rainfall occurred just within the last week of August. We were right at the start of that last week.

Our complacency with having walked four months without camping in the rain a single night meant most of us were not prepared for a month's worth of rain in one week. I myself had been carrying an old rain jacket with holes in it and a pack cover buried so far into the depths of my pack that I had forgotten I even owned one. I was desperately lacking in sufficient warm clothes. Outside of what I was wearing, I had a thinly insulated jacket and a beanie. I also had a lightweight pair of polyester liner gloves. They were about as thick as a pair of silk stockings. No long johns, no fleece pants or jackets, no warm socks and I had gotten rid of my umbrella months before due to ridicule from my fellow hikers. I would have given up my college diploma for that umbrella right now.

"My tent flooded a bit," Trim shouted over the roaring noise of the pouring onslaught early the next morning.

I peaked out from under the bottom of my tent and could see Honolulu packing up.

"What's the plan guys?" I asked from inside the friendly confines of my spacious and dry two-man tent.

"I don't know but I'm packing up and heading out of here stat," Honolulu said with a slight sense of urgency that made me think I should be doing the same.

Frankly though, I had absolutely no desire to do anything but stay in my sleeping bag. Perhaps I'd boil some water and have a steaming cup of tea or go back to sleep or both. Packing up a wet tent and trudging down a muddy trail in a cold downpour was at the bottom of my to do list.

After both Honolulu and Trim hiked out, I quickly decided that hanging out in my tent all day around a lonely lake with bad weather didn't seem that appealing. The rain had momentarily softened from full gale to downpour, which gave me the best opportunity I'd seen all morning to break camp. I grudgingly unzipped my sleeping bag and packed up everything inside my tent. I put on a pair of non-waterproof wind pants over my hiking shorts because that's all I had and it looked way too nasty to be walking around in running shorts. All I had on the top half of my body was a long sleeved shirt and a thrashed rain jacket. I put on my flimsy liner gloves, hustled out of my tent and packed the soaking wet jumble of nylon into the big mesh pocket on the outside of my pack.

I hiked out in the downpour. My wind pants were soaked within ten minutes. They clung to my damp skin like a sandwich wrapper to a soggy BLT. I had to wipe my sunglasses every three minutes just to see where I was going. It was ludicrous I even had them on in the first place, but I had surmised they would deflect some of the blowing rain. My liner gloves absorbed water like a dish sponge. I stuck my soaking wet hands into the soaking wet pockets of my soaking wet pants and started to shiver a bit as I hiked on. I had only been on the trail for thirty minutes. This was not good.

Our next "town stop" along the PCT wouldn't be a town at all. It would be the remote outpost that is Ollalie Lake Resort. Ollalie Lake Resort was the fourth or fifth resort we had come across during our jaunt through Oregon on the PCT. The term "resort" conjures up images of the clear warm waters and sunny beaches of the Caribbean. Perhaps snorkeling along the Keys while dining on fresh caught flounder or mahi mahi at night. A Swedish massage, maybe, or expensive dark chocolates lying on the pillow of a king size bed in the master suite. The Oregon resorts were a bit different. They were located in rural areas typically abutting National Forest land and most contained dated wooden cabins, pay showers and restaurants with an assortment of fried foods and an abundant supply of second-hand smoke. There were definitely not any dark chocolates on the pillows . . . there weren't even pillows. I had neither high hopes nor any hope that Ollalie would provide much in the way of salvation for my cohorts and I.

I sheltered briefly under a large pine, which reduced the downpour to only a steady rain. I pulled out my guidebook with a bit of effort to see how far Ollalie Lake Resort was from Rockpile Lake - 33 miles. This was a colossal distance by most standards. We had been hiking around 25 miles per day, which normally took us all day. I didn't even know if 33 miles was possible. That's equivalent to running a marathon and then tacking on a 10k afterwards. And we weren't running; we were hiking with heavy backpacks in the pouring rain on a trail that had become so muddy that what we were doing would be better described as careening.

I started to shiver and decided that I needed more clothes on my upper body ASAP. I could have gone for an Eskimo's parka with hood and waterproof shell but my thinly insulated jacket would have to work. I dug down in my pack as water poured off the bill of my hat. I grabbed the insulated jacket and put it on as swiftly as possible and slapped my rain jacket back on over it without delay. I reached down to zip up my insulated jacket and simply couldn't. My fingers wouldn't work. My brain was telling my hands to zip my jacket, but they simply could not grasp the zipper. I had lost all dexterity in my fingers. I couldn't zip my jacket and I was in a pouring cold rain. My hiking partners were up ahead so they had no clue as to what was happening to me. I was utterly alone in a torrential downpour and I couldn't zip my stupid jacket. A bolt of panic ran up from my stomach to my throat and for about 10 long seconds I thought about dying.

***

Hypothermia is defined as any body temperature below 95 °F (35 °C). There are three stages that take place as a person progresses from feeling chilly to greeting Saint Peter. Stage 1 is characterized by mild to strong shivering. The person is unable to perform complex tasks with the hands; the hands become numb (that was me). Blood vessels in the outer extremities constrict, lessening heat loss to the outside air. Breathing becomes quick and shallow. Goose bumps form, raising body hair on end in an attempt to create an insulating layer of air around the body (which is of limited use in humans due to lack of sufficient hair, but apparently useful in other species). Victims may feel sick to their stomachs, and very tired. People will often experience a warm sensation, as if they have recovered, but they are in fact heading into Stage 2.

Another test to see if one is entering stage 2 is if the person is unable to touch his thumb with his little finger; this is the first stage of muscles not working. I'm not sure if I could have touched my thumb to my pinky. I'm guessing not since I couldn't even clasp the zipper on my jacket.

In Stage 2 of hypothermia, body temperature drops as low as 91 °F (32 °C). Shivering becomes more violent. Muscle miscoordination becomes apparent. Movements are slow and labored, accompanied by a stumbling pace and mild confusion, although the person may appear alert. Surface blood vessels contract further as the body focuses its remaining resources on keeping the vital organs warm. The victim becomes pale. Lips, ears, fingers and toes may become blue. I never hit Stage 2 and I'll get to why in a moment.

Finally in Stage 3, the body temperature drops below approximately 89.6 °F (32 °C). Shivering usually stops. Difficulty speaking, sluggish thinking, and amnesia start to appear; inability to use hands and stumbling is also usually present. Cellular metabolic processes shut down. Below 86.0 °F (30 °C), the exposed skin becomes blue and puffy, muscle coordination becomes very poor, walking becomes almost impossible, and is typically accompanied by irrational behavior including terminal burrowing (an odd phenomenon where the hypothermia victim burrows into leaves or rock crevices as a protection mechanism). Pulse and respiration rates decrease significantly, but fast heart rates (ventricular tachycardia, atrial fibrillation) can occur. Major organs fail. Clinical death occurs. Because of decreased cellular activity in Stage 3 hypothermia, the body will actually take longer to undergo brain death.

Realizing that my situation was serious, I decided to pull my rain jacket as close to my chest as possible, jam my wet hands in my wet pockets and hike as fast as I possibly could to generate heat. I kept a bit of a forward lean to shield the unzipped area of my rain jacket from falling raindrops. I was practically running down the trail. For the next 45 minutes I hustled as fast as I could and stayed focused on both generating body heat and rewarming my hands. By the time I stopped to zip my jacket I could see Honolulu and Trim up ahead. I pulled my hands out of my wind pants and zipped the zipper with no problem. Dexterity had come back to my fingers.

I caught up to Honolulu and Trim and told them about losing dexterity in my fingers, which they didn't seem to think was that big of a deal. Little did they know that I was on the verge of having a panic attack.

"I don't know what you guys are planning to do today, but I'm hiking all the way into Ollalie Lake before six o'clock when their store closes. I'm not camping out in the rain tonight," I declared.

Looking fairly drenched and low on proper gear and clothes themselves, they both said they were in. It was decided; we were going to attempt to lay down 33 miles in 10 hours in the pouring rain. We were on a mission, and in my mind, the consequence of not succeeding was hypothermia.

I don't remember a whole lot of the details of the next nine hours or so on the trail. It rained, it poured, it was windy, and foggy and the temperature never got much out of the low 40's. We were hiking through the spectacularly scenic Mt. Jefferson Wilderness and saw none of it. Honolulu later told me that he could barely keep up with me as I was practically running instead of hiking.

I took two breaks of five minutes each during the day, just long enough to wolf down an energy bar or two, but that was it. Frankly, I was too scared to stop. I assumed that if I stopped for more than five or ten minutes, I'd lose dexterity in my fingers again and shit creek would be my new home. I was absolutely bound and determined to get myself to Ollalie Lake where I knew I'd find salvation in the form of a cabin or yurt for rent. We had heard they had wood-burning stoves. The thought of sitting in front of a warm wood-burning stove wearing dry clothes drinking a piping hot cup of chai was almost too much to handle.

At fifteen minutes before six o'clock, we reached a dirt road with a large wooden sign that pointed the way to Ollalie Lake Resort. Within minutes we slogged inside the camp store to pay for accommodations for the evening. I was in awe that we had covered 33 miles in less than ten hours but that was going to have to wait. We needed to pay for our cabin ASAP and get into dryer clothes.

"How much for a cabin tonight?" I asked the store clerk.

"I'm sorry but we are full. There was a big party here last night and all the cabins and yurts have been booked for the entire weekend," the clerk told me.

I was completely crushed - completely and utterly crushed. It was still dumping rain and it would be dark in an hour or so. I wanted to tell the guy that I had been borderline hypothermic earlier that day and that I deserved a cabin way more than the party boys from the previous night.

"Do you have any other lodging options that involve a covered roof," I stammered.

"Not today. Something might open up tomorrow. You are more then welcome to camp in the resort campground across the road," he replied. "We've got free hot chocolate," he said, trying to lift our spirits as he pointed to a small thermos by the counter.

I poked my head out the door of the store to look over at the campground. It was a dismal affair in a low spot full of puddles and mud. It didn't have any trees and was completely exposed to the rain. It was bleak. It was grim. And it wasn't going to work.

I walked back in the store and talked to Honolulu and Trim. They had the same look of rejection and despair on their faces as I was sure that I had on mine. What in the name of all that is holy and good were we going to do? I felt low – really, really low - similar to the day that I found out an old fling I was head over heels for had dumped me like a bag of bricks for a guy that was 10 years younger than me.

Honolulu suggested that we should buy as much hot food as possible before the store closed. He found some microwave burritos and the three of us commenced warming them while sipping on some of the complimentary hot chocolate. I tried to convince myself that tonight would be fine but that thought was fleeting and I went back to anguish rather quickly. We were screwed and it was going to be a cold, wet night in a cold, wet campsite.

At that very moment, "Trainwreck," "Strut" and "Jupiter" burst through the door of the store. They had arrived the day before and decided to take the day off because the weather was so dour. We had hiked on and off with these three girls since the southern California desert and it was great to see them.

"What are you guys doing?" Trainwreck asked.

"We're trying to get some food as quickly as possible before the store closes. And then we're going out in that shitty camp-site across the road to set up for the night," I said with defeat.

"No you're not. We've got a warm, dry cabin with a wood-burning stove and you all are staying with us," she said matter of factly. I had never gone from such a low point to such a high point in such a short span of time in my entire life. My eyes welled up with tears and I asked her if she was serious. She said yes and to grab our stuff so we could go.

I couldn't believe how our luck had changed in a matter of seconds. I was mentally preparing for one of the worst nights of my life while trying to heat a cheap microwave burrito in hopes that it would provide some scant glimpse of salvation. And it was only moments before the store closed at which time we would be forced back out into the rainy, dreary, hypothermic weather. With the blink of an eye, all that changed. We had been rescued by Trainwreck, Strut and Jupiter. I've never been so grateful for someone taking pity on me in my entire life.

I looked back at the store clerk with a brief glance. He had held our fragile state of being in his hands and had told us there was no place to stay with the neutrality of a Swiss banker. He had no idea what we had gone through that day. None. I felt if only he had known, he would have found us a warm, dry place to stay. Likely I was partially delirious to feel that this guy who was pulling down minimum wage at best had the key to the world, but that's how it seemed during our ten minutes in the store. And now it didn't matter. We didn't need this guy any longer. Our fellow hikers had come to save us from the elements. So long, sucker.

Before heading back to their cabin for the night, we found out that they had all been invited over to the staff cabin for a concert of sorts. Apparently one of the staffers had graduated from the Berklee College of Music with a degree in Composition and was an amazing classical guitarist. The staff house was warm and cozy with the smell of a wood-burning stove. Over the next hour, Grant serenaded our crew with a piece that left us all in a trance. It was amazing. I sat there on the floor with ten other thru-hikers in a warm house listening to a free concert while it poured rain outside. Only ten short hours prior, I had been standing in the middle of the trail with the early stages of hypothermia trying to zip a jacket with fingers that would not work. I was in awe of how the day had panned out and so happy that we had been rescued and brought to the staff cabin for a classical guitar performance.

After our guitar concerto, we all piled in one of the staffers trucks and he gave us a ride back to our cabin. Somehow yesterday, Trainwreck and Co. were able to score a cabin for rent that was three miles from the main resort. This happened after they had been told everything else was booked for the entire weekend.

The cabin was a rustic, large A-frame roughly 20' by 15' with a huge wood-burning stove and loft that contained a couple of bunks. With 12 people in there it got warm fast. From one end to the other there were clotheslines draped with gear and wet rain jackets and pants hung out to dry. "Captain Mike," another hiker in our crew of 12, took it upon himself to keep the fire going all night. He'd get up every couple of hours or so to add a couple of logs.

The next morning came early as they always do when you're sleeping in close quarters with a dozen people. The early risers were up and fidgeting around before the day had even dawned. Honolulu, Trim and I hiked out late morning, a bit after everyone else. We were moving slowly. My legs felt like linguine. I guess walking 33 miles in 10 hours with two five-minute breaks was more than the two ibuprofen pills I had taken the night before could handle.

I picked up an extra campers poncho at the resort store with the hopes that it would help my lack of legitimate rain-proof gear and clothing. We spent the next four days making our way up and around Mt. Hood and down to the town of Cascade Locks along the Columbia River. There a short ride to Portland from my friend Kate gave us quick access to every outfitter and gear store under the sun. I probably overdid it with my purchases, not ever wanting to head down that sad, soggy road to hypothermia again. My pack was a bit heavier with an assortment of raingear for that final month on the trail, but I didn't care. It rained three out of every four days for the rest of the hike and I never again found myself too cold to zip a jacket.

4

Of Mice and Men

There comes a point on every long hike where the will to continue no longer exists. Sometimes these moments are fleeting. Sometimes they last weeks and are enough to send you looking for the nearest Greyhound station. When things get bad, and typically it's a mental bad in addition to a physical bad, you can convince yourself that any other possible endeavor in the world would be better than continuing your hike. Things like going back to a job you hated, going back to a significant other you left, taking that underwater basket weaving course you had previously considered pointless or any host of other aspirations that weren't even on your radar a week ago now seem urgent.

There is much in the way of adversity on a 2,000+ mile hike, some real and some perceived. There's heat, cold, rain, snow, humidity, ants, flies, gnats, mosquitoes, wildfires, bears, mountain lions, porcupines, skunks (yes skunks), tarantulas, scorpions, a surplus of poisonous snakes, deer flies, horse flies, black flies, yellow jackets, hornets, giardia, cryptosporidia, Montezuma's revenge, Lyme disease, Rocky Mountain spotted fever, babesiosis, Colorado tick fever, ehrliciosis, West Nile virus, eastern equine encephalitis, plague, hantavirus, staph infections, chafing, blisters, boils, poison ivy, poison oak, poison sumac, allergies, loneliness, home sickness and a broken heart to name a few. Any one of these misfortunes usually is surmountable. The problem comes when you get multiple hardships occurring at the same time for weeks on end. They slowly chip away at you until you break.

On the Appalachian Trail in 1999, I had hiked from Georgia to Connecticut . . . some 1,500 miles and almost ¾ of the trail's length and mentally I was done. It had been incredibly hot for multiple weeks - mid-90's everyday and humidity so thick you could swim through it, like hiking through molasses. Thick, sticky, syrupy molasses. The mosquitoes were relentless and attempted to drain my blood whenever I stopped moving and stood still for more than a half second. This went on for weeks. I was lonely too. I missed my girlfriend more than I can tell you and was wondering why anyone in their right minds would voluntarily choose to be out here right now trudging up and down hillsides, swatting mosquitoes and deer flies in 96 degree heat?

On July 4th, I camped by myself at Pine Swamp Branch Lean-to, a three-sided shelter in a lowly spot surrounded by marshy vegetation somewhere in western Connecticut. The nighttime temp got down to 73. As I lay in my tent as still as possible completely in the buff hoping for any type of breeze to waft through and cool me down, I could hear the sound of fireworks going off in the distance. For hours the bang and pop of great Fourth of July celebrations rang in my ears. I had visions of cheery people standing around barbeques, stuffing their faces with smoked pork, coleslaw and potato chips while drinking from kegs of ice-cold beer. They were high fiving their buddies and oohing and aahing over the roman candles and bottle rockets making their way skyward. And they would retire in a few hours to cool and comfortable air-conditioned homes, completely oblivious to the heat and bugs that had taken over the great outdoors where I resided.

I could do nothing but lay there and listen to the high pitched whine of half a million mosquitoes that would do anything to grow fingers with opposable thumbs to unzip my tent door and come in to dine. Why was I out here? What was I doing? Any remnant of the excitement and anticipation that I had that fateful day back in March when I set off from Springer Mountain to walk the Appalachian Trail to Maine was gone. I was well behind my self-imposed schedule by some two weeks and had been skipping town stops to try and catch up. I was trampled and beaten both physically and mentally. I was ready to quit.

The next morning I gathered my gear, packed as quickly as possible while swatting mosquitoes, and literally ran out of Pine Swamp. By the time I reached Highway 44, I knew that I needed to do whatever I had to do to get off the trail. I needed a few days off to evaluate my decision to quit. I ran into a few AT Ridgerunners in Salisbury who agreed to give me a ride to the town of Kent. Once in Kent I called my friend "Dogman" who was also thru-hiking the AT that summer. His parents lived near Kent and he had been taking some time off to recoup at their house. Within 30 minutes he picked me up in front of the local outfitters and whisked me back to his house. I was filthy dirty and smelled like a cattle pen.

We pulled up in his driveway and I immediately noticed the sparkling clear swimming pool in his backyard. Without hesitation I shut the door to his car, walked over to the pool and jumped in with all my clothes on. The cold pool water was possibly the most refreshing thing I had ever experienced in my entire life. I spent the next three hours in the pool just sitting there soaking my body and chlorinating my vile hiker garb. I devoted the better part of the next two days to Dogman's pool. It literally changed everything. The heat wave broke and I got back on the trail a few days later right where I had left off and hiked to Maine.

In the end I didn't need to quit the AT. I simply wanted to because I was physically worn out by the heat and mosquitoes and had beaten myself up mentally about being behind schedule (schedules are for the workaday world and it was ridiculous that I had brought this taskmaster mentality onto the trail in the first place). I had convinced myself that I could no longer go on. All I really needed was a bit of time off . . . in a pool . . . out of the heat and the bugs. I needed some time away from the madness to regain my perspective on why I was out there. My two days at Dogman's did exactly that and when I hit the trail again, I couldn't help but wonder what I had made such a fuss about.

Most hikers experience some type of low point like this while hiking for months on end. It's almost inevitable. It's not always butterflies and rainbows. Quite the contrary. My friend "Buck-30," a seasoned long-distance hiker, developed a rating system during his CDT thru-hike in 2005 . . . a misery index of sorts. He concluded simply that there were six specific things that really pissed him off on the CDT:

1. Bugs
2. No Existing Trail
3. Hot Sun
4. No Water/Cow Shit Water
5. Allergies
6. Very Steep Trail

He told me that any of these by themselves or paired with one other was no big deal. Basically these things were more or less to be expected while hiking in the summer. Three of them at once meant things were getting tough, four is rough, five really pissed him off and six made him cry. And if you're curious about the "Cow Shit Water," well that's exactly what he's talking about: water sources fouled and polluted by cattle herds dumping directly into them. Sometimes that was the only water available for miles on end. Bottoms up!

The day he came up with this index, he was at the tail end of Montana on the CDT during a 2005 southbound thru-hike from Canada to Mexico. Oddly enough, I would find myself at a breaking point almost a year later at the same exact spot.

2006 was the year that P.O.D. and I decided to attempt a CDT thru-hike heading southbound. We figured it would be easier than going northbound since northbounders are racing winter from the moment they set foot on the trail. Northbounders finish in Glacier National Park and sometimes winter shows up in mid-September and doesn't leave until June. Most "nobos" start at the Mexican Border around May 1st, which gives them roughly 4 ½ months to get to Canada. Anything longer than 4 ½ months puts them in Glacier after mid-September. That's rolling the dice. The further past mid-September it gets, the more likely Glacier will be closed down for the season due to snow. I've known hikers who showed up a bit late and ended up walking road shoulders the last week of their hikes just to get to Canada.

As a southbounder or "sobo," your main goal is to get down through Colorado before the snow really starts to fly in the Centennial state's southernmost mountain range . . . the San Juans. The San Juan Mountains typically get the highest snowfall of any mountain range in Colorado during a given year. Think 500 inches or more. That's 42 feet. It can snow in the San Juans any month of the year and does. Most of the time the real snow stays at bay until October and sometimes even November. As a sobo, the goal is to get through Colorado and the San Juans by October 1st. Once you hit New Mexico, you can lollygag your way down to the finish in the lower and warmer climes of the Land of Enchantment.

We thought the "lollygagging at the end" part would be nice so we started our hike at the Canadian Border in mid-June, which is when the majority of sobos start their hikes. The main problem with starting at the Canadian border in mid-June and hiking 800 miles through Montana in July is that it's usually hot and usually buggy. 2006 was unusually hot and unusually buggy. It was the third hottest summer on record ever in Montana. The heat multiplies the bugs. We had deer flies, horse flies and mosquitoes. At the end of every day P.O.D. and I would vote which of the three got the "Bug of the Day Award." The award would go to the most proliferate pest that annoyed us during the past 24 hours. Some days we would have trouble choosing because two of the three had been dreadful all day. Every once in a while it would be all three.

Looking at Buck-30's misery index above, we experienced Category 4's or 5's on almost all of the 48 days it took us to walk the CDT through Montana. So much for butterflies and rainbows. By the time we reached Wyoming, we were on edge and a bit worn down. I had lost 15 pounds and simply couldn't consume enough calories to replace the ones I was burning on a daily basis. There's so much up and down on the CDT in Montana. Many days would bring 5,000 feet of up and 5,000 feet of down. That's like walking the stairwell of a 500 story building to the top and then walking 500 stories back down in one fell swoop. The Empire State Building is only 102 stories high.

There's a spot in northern Wyoming called "Parting of the Waters." Hikers walk right down to it as they cross Two Ocean Creek. The creek splits in two around a large spruce tree. The jet on the west side eventually makes its way into the Pacific Ocean while the jet on the east side eventually gets itself to the Gulf of Mexico and then the Atlantic Ocean. Just before we reached Two Ocean Creek, we stopped to take a quick snack break near a small brook. We had been hiking with a girl named "Lovebarge" who constantly had us in stitches and she stopped to take a break with us.

After twenty minutes of lounging, I wasn't feeling too motivated to get up from our break spot. As P.O.D. packed up to head out, I sat there on a log not wanting to go anywhere. Even the lure of Two Ocean Creek and the famous "Parting of the Waters" was not enough to make me budge. P.O.D. took about ten steps and mumbled something about a dead mouse. I didn't pay much attention until I saw a grey blur arcing through the air towards Lovebarge and I. This was enough to make me budge and I jumped up from my seat on the log and took five steps back. The dead mouse landed on my Gossamer Gear Mariposa backpack.

This might not seem like a big deal but it broke my will in half. I was more than a bit worn down both physically and mentally from our hike through Montana. I had incorrectly assumed that the rest of the CDT would be as tough as the previous 48 days (it was not). I was mentally trying to wrap my brain around hiking another three and a half months under similar brutality. I hadn't done much to convey any of the misgivings and doubt that had crept into my brain to P.O.D. so she had no idea of my fragile state. And when she flung the dead mouse off the tip of her hiking pole in our general direction, she had not intended for it to hit either of us or our packs. But it did and it simply crushed me.

It didn't help that I'm a bit of a clean freak too. I'll admit it. Even on trail, I like to stay as clean as possible. I carry wet wipes for a refreshing wash at the end of each day on the trail. For years I've also carried a blue dish sponge for which I've been made fun of relentlessly by other hikers. I use it to sponge bathe once or twice a day while on trail. It does absolute wonders for keeping me semi-clean and not feeling like a filthy vagabond. Some hikers carry extra chocolate, some carry a MP3 player . . . I carry a dish sponge.

The mouse that landed on my pack was partially rotted. It had been dead for days as it slowly decayed on the stream's edge. As with any animal decay, various types of bugs and critters usually appear to help speed the process. When the mouse landed on my pack, the impact propelled a few of the maggots that were consuming it onto the bare nylon near my backpack's side pockets. I simply stared at this scene in mild horror and utter disbelief. I was in the middle of Bridger-Teton National Forest with no running water in sight, days from the nearest town, miles to go before days end, with a dead mouse and live maggots on my pack. I couldn't just walk over to the side of my house, grab the hose and rinse it off, nor could I walk over to the sink in my garage, turn the hot water on and soap it up. I could do none of these things. I would have to improvise. I didn't want to improvise though, I wanted to quit, to go home. I wanted to leave the pack exactly where it lay on the ground with the dead mouse and maggots and walk to a Greyhound Station, buy a ticket to anywhere and leave. I had been holding on by a thread and this mouse just broke that thread.

P.O.D. looked at me expressionless, knowing that what had just happened was bad. Lovebarge broke into hysterics and laughed for the next thirty minutes. She even pulled out her camera and took photos of my reaction. I summoned a laugh but what I really wanted to do was lie on the ground and cry . . . and then go catch the first train to Yuma.

P.O.D. ran over to me and apologized profusely as Lovebarge snapped photos. She removed the mouse with a couple of dead branches lying nearby and took my pack down to the creek and rinsed it off. I took a bit of hand sanitizer that I carried with my toilet paper and did my best at sanitizing the oily mouse/maggot remnants on my pack.

Lovebarge hiked out chortling while P.O.D. and I hung back to finish the clean up. Over the next half hour, I explained to P.O.D. that I was ready to quit. I told her that things like what just happened simply could not happen again. I just couldn't handle it. I was at my breaking point and ready to call it good for the summer and head home.

After venting all my woes and self-doubts to P.O.D., I immediately felt better. I did need a break though. A few days in a hotel at minimum - a quick week at Club Med preferably. We checked over our budget and decided that Club Med was not in the cards. We hiked for two more days and got a ride into the small town of Dubois, Wyoming. Dubois had an abundance of restaurants and hotels. I sampled most of the restaurants and spent the rest of my time lounging around the Black Bear Inn with my feet propped up and the air conditioning cranked to the arctic breeze setting. It was sheer bliss and exactly what I needed to get my head back on straight.

I sat in the hotel room and thought about the mouse incident above Two Ocean Creek. Ridiculous, really. It was easy to think those thoughts now as I lay horizontal on a soft mattress, the air conditioner keeping the room to just above an ice box level, not a bug in sight . . . or a mouse. I was even able to catch a marathon showing of my favorite on trail hotel room TV programming, *Dog the Bounty Hunter*. This wasn't Club Med - but it was relief.

Two days later we saddled up, loaded our packs and hit the trail again. We were heading into Wyoming's famed Wind River Range. The "Winds," as they are called, contain Wyoming's highest peak - Gannet Peak, at 13,804 feet - and 40 other named peaks above 13,000 feet. They run for approximately 100 miles and are comprised mostly of granite. I don't know if it was the granite or the cooler high elevation temps, but the bugs disappeared and the heat became a forgotten memory as we traipsed around this range on top of the world.

A world-renowned trail runner and snowshoe racer once gave me some really good advice on the eve of running my first marathon. He said that it's gonna get bad at some point but "don't project ahead." With running a marathon, it's not uncommon to hit mile 19 or 20 and feel like complete garbage. A mile or two later you'll find yourself feeling good again. You just need to push through the tough miles to get back to the effortless ones. That advice holds true on the trail and I wish someone had told me this little nugget of wisdom back at Two Ocean Creek. Don't project ahead . . . it will get better. And it did.

5

Gator-Boy

I felt giddy as I walked up the street from Shaw's Boarding House to the post office in the sleepy hamlet of Monson, Maine. I had done this ritual time and time again in trail towns from Georgia to Maine all along the Appalachian Trail. This time was different because Monson was the last town with a post office before reaching the northern terminus and finish of the AT – Mt. Katahdin (pronounced Ka-Tah-Den).

Picking up maildrops is the hiker equivalent of Christmas morning. You never know what you are going to get or from whom but it is always a surprise and usually puts a smile on your face.

The small post office in Monson was similar to other trail town post offices I had visited over the last five months. Compact, just the basics, one clerk and no line.

"I've got some packages General Delivery," I told the clerk, handing her my South Carolina driver's license.

"Thru-hiking?" she asked.

"Yep. Almost done. Hard to believe," I said.

She smiled and headed into the back of the building where a separate pile of hiker packages stood stacked almost to the ceiling. I watched, wondering just what goodies I'd receive.

"Here ya go," she said as she pushed a pile of mail to my side of the counter.

I walked out of the post office with three letters, two boxes and one small package. After hustling back to my tent on the lawn at Shaw's Boarding House, I started going through all the packages and letters one by one. Letters from my grandma and sister. A box from my dad. A box from Mom. And a small package from Betty Cram. In Betty's package were a letter and a film canister.

Betty was the mother of a friend of mine from college. Jake "Gator-Boy" Cram lived next door to my girlfriend during my junior year at Clemson University. Gator-Boy was a wild hair, but an all around stand-up guy. He moonlighted on weekends as a snow ski instructor at Ski Beech in western North Carolina. I first got the idea of skiing in a business suit from him - although he took a different tact, dressing up as Cosmo Kramer from *Seinfeld* or a character he called "Silver Man" while moving at obscenely high speed down the runs of Ski Beech. "There's nothing that upsets beginning skiers more than when they get left in the dust by some jackass in a silver suit," he told me.

Jake and I got to be friends during that year in college and he keyed me in on a little known academic delight . . . leisure skills courses. Clemson had everything from rock climbing, to ballroom dancing, to sailing, bowling and even backpacking. We both signed up for LS 182 that Spring Semester - Backpacking and Camping, a 1-hour credit.

On one of the mandatory overnight backpacking trips we did as part of our class, Jake told me that he planned to hike the Appalachian Trail after he graduated in May. He showed me a full-length wall poster of the Appalachian Trail and I was blown away. I had hiked a small section of the AT before in both Georgia and North Carolina during an Outward Bound course at the age of 16, but I did not fully comprehend that the trail ran from Georgia to Maine as one continuous footpath until I gawked at that map.

I asked him all the standard questions that a person asks an AT thru-hiker:

"How much will the hike cost?"

"Where do you buy food?"

"Do you get to take a shower?"

"Does a bear really shit in the woods?"

He had answers for everything I fired at him. Jake told me that hikers go into towns near the trail once or twice a week to buy groceries, get a hotel room, shower and recoup from all the dusty miles. He also told me his mom was going to send him pre-packaged maildrops full of food at a lot of these town stops.

I asked him if he had a list of the towns he would stop in and an idea of when he'd be there. He handed over a spreadsheet of towns and places I had never heard of before:

Hiawassee, Georgia
Damascus, Virginia
Harper's Ferry, West Virginia
Boiling Springs, Pennsylvania
Bear Mountain, New York
Killington, Vermont
Gorham, New Hampshire

Jake started his hike near the AT's halfway point, Harper's Ferry, WV. He planned to hike from Harper's Ferry north to Maine and then get a ride back to Harper's Ferry and hike down to Georgia. In the long-distance hiking world, this type of hike is known as a "flip-flop" and made sense because he would get a late start due to a May college graduation.

Most folks that hike the entire AT from Georgia to Maine start in March or April with hopes of getting to Maine before

Katahdin closes in October. Hikers heading southbound from Maine to Georgia typically start in late June or July and push to get down to Georgia before winter really sets in.

On June 1st, 1997, Gator-Boy started his AT thru-hike with a friend from Clemson after being dropped off in Harper's Ferry by his parents. I got periodic postcards during those first few weeks on the trail.

A common malady many thru-hikers experience in the early going of a long-distance hike is the reality that a heavy pack full of heavy gear works against them. Jake sent me a postcard proclaiming, "On a long hike, you actually need less gear." This seems counterintuitive at first but it's quite true. Hiking with a 50-pound pack during a weekend excursion is no big deal because you'll be home and showered sometime Sunday night. Hiking with a 50-pound pack over the course of 5-6 months will make your life utterly miserable and possibly reduce your height by and inch or two!

Jake's starting pack weight was a spine compressing 70 pounds. By the end of his first month out there, Jake sent a lot of his gear home and cut his pack weight tremendously. He seemed to be hitting his stride by the time he got to Vermont. I'd been sending him candy bars and single serving Gatorade powder packets to the towns on his maildrop list. I figured that combo would be something any long-distance hiker could use.

***

I came home from summer school class that August day to find my girlfriend in tears and extremely distraught. My stomach knotted because I knew something was bad, bad wrong. She looked at me with tears streaming down her face and said, "Jake's dead."

"Jake who?" I asked in that odd moment of not comprehending the gravity of the situation.

"Jake Cram."

I sat down on the cement steps in front of my apartment in disbelief. I was thunderstruck.

"What happened?"

"Nobody knows yet. They haven't done an autopsy. All Marcia told me was that he collapsed on the trail in New Hampshire and died."

Emily continued sobbing as I tried to process what she had just told me. How could this be possible? Jake was 22 years old. People our age didn't just collapse and die. This couldn't be right. This had to be a mistake.

Just a few days before, on August 19th, Jake had hiked into the Liberty Tentsite on his way up from Franconia Notch to Franconia Ridge in New Hampshire's White Mountains. Gator-Boy told the caretaker there that he had suffered from a migraine all day and was feeling ill. The caretaker offered to let Jake stay at the tent site overnight for free given his condition. During the night Jake got up a number of times to throw up. Assuming he had some type of mild food poisoning and still feeling bad, he didn't give much thought to hiking out the next morning. It's pretty standard for thru-hikers to push on while they are sick. On more than one occasion that I have seen hikers nearly fall over due to giardiasis, shin splints, food poisoning, staph infections and trench foot but continue on because they just "had to keep going."

By lunchtime he was above tree line and had crested the top of Mt. Lincoln. Within an hour of being on Lincoln, he laid out his sleeping pad, pulled out his sleeping bag, got in it and zipped it up. Odd behavior for the middle of an afternoon on a warm August day in the White Mountains.

A high school teacher from Conway, New Hampshire out on a day hike saw Jake on the side of the trail and stopped to see what was going on. Within minutes, another hiker, Brad Sturgis, arrived to find the schoolteacher talking to a dazed Jake.

Sally Sotheby had been on a day hike with her aunt, aunt's husband, uncle and cousin that morning as a weekend get-a-way. Sally's mom dropped them all off at the Lafayette Place Campground trailhead around 9:00 A.M. They were planning to hike up to Mt. Lafayette via the Old Bridle Path and then back down to the trailhead on the Falling Waters Trail – a classic New England day hike with mind-blowing above tree line views.

They made quick work of the trail getting up to Mt. Lafayette and were headed over to Mt. Lincoln and onto Little Haystack Mountain to catch the Falling Waters Trail back down. Sally had been ahead of her family when they reached Mt. Lincoln at 3:00 P.M. and she was startled when she came upon Jake in his sleeping bag with two concerned hikers tending to him.

"Is he ok?" she asked the schoolteacher, a bit concerned.

"He's a bit dehydrated and has a migraine," the teacher replied. "We sent a note for help to the staff at the Greenleaf Hut with some day hikers."

The rest of Sally's family showed up and decided to take a break there and see if they could be of some assistance.

Jake was in and out of consciousness and at 3:30, he had a mild seizure. At this point, Brad decided that he would hike to Greenleaf Hut himself to let the staff there know how serious Jake's condition was.

Brad hustled the 2-½ miles to Greenleaf Hut. Greenleaf is one of eight Appalachian Mountain Club (AMC) huts spread throughout White Mountain National Forest along the Appalachian Trail. Huts vary in capacity and can accommodate 36 to 90 overnight guests depending on their size. They cater to hikers who want to sleep indoors while still getting a taste of the outdoors and they allow hikers to trek hut to hut without having to carry much gear, similar to hut systems in the Alps. More importantly, these huts are staffed with folks that have wilderness first aid and emergency medical training.

Somewhat panicked and without wasting a second, Brad immediately told the hut crew at Greenleaf about Jake's condition. Two members of the crew headed out the door en route to Jake within 10 minutes of meeting Brad.

Sally, her cousin Jay, her Uncle Charlie and the teacher all decided to stay with Jake until help arrived. Sally's aunt and her aunt's husband headed out for the trailhead to let Sally's mom know that those staying with Jake would be delayed and would likely not make it back before dark.

They covered the ground from the Hut to Jake in less than an hour and arrived around 6:00 P.M. This was no small feat considering the rocky, exposed terrain up and over Mt. Lafayette to get to Mt. Lincoln. Jake was semi-coherent when they reached him. A series of questions to Jake indicated to them that they needed to get Jake back to the Hut as soon as possible.

"Jake, I want you to drink this tea and have a granola bar," said Fred Smith, one of the Greenleaf Hut crew members.

"OK," replied Jake.

"Jake, we are going to help you hike to Greenleaf Hut. You're staying there tonight with us free of charge. How's that sound?" Fred asked.

"OK," Jake replied in a weak voice.

Fred and Phyllis Baker, the other hut crewmember present, helped Jake pack up. Jake had trouble standing upright and was helped by Kate and her family. Fred shouldered Jake's pack while Jake was getting ready for the hike out.

"So we are going to head down the trail. Just follow me. Phyllis will be right behind you," Fred proclaimed to a woozy Jake.

They all headed off at a slow walk. Jake was putting one foot in front of the other, which was about all they could ask for. 50 yards later Jake collapsed in a seizure in the middle of the trail. He stopped breathing and had no pulse. They began CPR and continued for over half an hour rechecking Jake's vitals at frequent intervals. Jake never regained consciousness.

At 8:30 the next morning, a rescue team of 50 volunteers was convened. Personnel from the Androscoggin Valley Search and Rescue, Upper Valley Wilderness Rescue, Mountain Rescue, SOLO school and the AMC headed up to Mt. Lincoln to bring Jake's body off the mountain. The weather had turned overnight and rescuers faced foggy, misty conditions that changed over to blowing rains with winds gusting upwards of 70 mph. It was an all-day effort under foul weather conditions, but rescuers were able to get Jake's body down the mountain to Littleton Hospital in Grafton County.

An autopsy would later reveal that Jake had an undiagnosed tumor the size of a walnut inside his brain. The tumor caused a cerebral hemorrhage, which led to Jake's collapse on the trail.

***

Jake's parents, Richard and Betty, held a memorial hike for Jake the following summer on Mt. Lincoln. I was on my way from Oregon back to Rhode Island after spending three months working for the Forest Service on the Oregon coast. I met

Jake's family and friends in New Hampshire and we all headed up the AT from Franconia Notch the following morning.

I had never set foot on the AT north of the Nantahala River in western North Carolina, nor had I ever done any hiking in the White Mountains of New Hampshire, so this was entirely new terrain for me. We hiked up the two and a half miles from Franconia Notch to Liberty Tentsite where Jake spent his last night. From there it would be almost three miles to Mt. Lincoln. The total elevation gain was over 3,500', which was a steep climb and made the going slow and tough.

I was trying to imagine what was going through Jake's mind on that trek up to Mt. Lincoln. I imagined his migraine kept him from focusing on much of anything. And here on this morning a year later, it was a nice summer's day and the sun was out, there was a light wind and everything was green. It just didn't seem right that Jake wasn't here with us.

Over the course of the day I met a few thru-hikers. Most had heard about Gator-Boy and what had happened on Mt. Lincoln the previous summer. After a few hours we eventually crested a ridge and made it to the exposed knob that was Mt. Lincoln. We had a special ceremony and Betty spread his ashes over that rocky promenade on the Franconia Ridge.

After a quiet lunch, we all hiked back to Franconia Notch via the Falling Waters Trail and arrived just before dark. I leaned back on my daypack to wait for the rest of the group as they made their way down this steep trail. It had been an emotional day. I thought of the thru-hikers I had met. I thought of Jake and his family. And I had an overwhelming feeling that was as clear as day . . . I felt compelled to hike the AT. It's as if it wasn't even a question open for discussion; the decision had been made. Next year I would set out from Springer and follow in Jake's footsteps.

I opened the package from Betty Cram to find a letter and a film canister. The letter read:

Dear Lawton,

Good for you! Your last maildrop! Now into the "100 mile wilderness." I hope it's a great hike and you have good companions.

I never was able to talk to you since "Trail Days" to ask about sending the things I am now. I hope it is alright and does not interfere with your enjoyment of your accomplishment.

I would have loved so much to bring these things to Mt. Katahdin myself but don't know if I ever will get to and I don't want to keep waiting to bring some of Jake's ashes there. And if someday I do, that'll be ok too. Take Jake to the top for us!

If you don't want to carry his ashes you could mail them back to me before leaving Monson.

Richard says, "Enjoy the Moment," although he says he believes most AT hikers are often in the moment just by circumstance.

Let us know when you finish. Take us some photos!

Love and Best Wishes, the Crams (Betty & Richard)

Tears welled up in my eyes as I lifted the lid on the enclosed film canister to see Jake's ashes. I closed the lid and knew without a doubt that it would be an honor to carry his ashes through the 100-Mile Wilderness and up Katahdin. I wouldn't be here in Monson, Maine right now if it weren't for Jake.

In addition to the letter and film canister was a single-serve packet of orange Gatorade. I had sent this packet of Gatorade to Gorham, New Hampshire, for Jake to pick up during his thru-hike. Gorham sits at the end of the Whites and Jake never made it there. Betty found it after all his unclaimed mail had been returned to them. Here I was two years later holding it in my hand. I decided that I would drink it on my way up Katahdin my last day on the trail.

A number of us hiked out of Shaw's the next morning and headed into the formidable 100-Mile Wilderness, one of the most remote sections of the AT. This stretch of trail would cross only a handful of roads and a sign at its start warned us to dare not enter unless we had 10 days worth of food. I had five and was planning on doing 20-mile days to get from one end to the other. The going was tough but a small group of us made it through in that time frame without a hitch. One of those hikers in that group was my friend "Grubby," a good guy from Michigan that I'd been hiking with on and off since Vermont. I told Grubby about my friend Gator-Boy and the container of ashes I was carrying.

Grubby was with me that last day on the trail. The day we all summitted Katahdin to finish a journey most of us had started five months prior down in Georgia. The climb up Katahdin gains 4,000 vertical feet in 5.2 miles. It's the biggest climb on the entire AT. Halfway up I refilled my water bottle from a cascading stream and mixed in the contents of the orange Gatorade packet. I sat down beside the stream for a few moments and thought about Gator-Boy. I knew he was there with me.

Grubby sent out a letter to a number of his friends chronicling that last day on the trail. It reads like this:

On August 26th, I was awakened by the scurrying of small animals outside of my tent. To say that the mice of the Appalachian Trail are pests would be an understatement. These are not ordinary rodents - they are "Super Mice", laughing at the meager defenses of our food bags and attacking our granola and gorp with abandon.

A glance at my watch revealed the time to be just after midnight. This was unfortunate as I knew that sleep would not return. The summit of Mt. Katahdin lay a mere 7.6 miles away and even in the darkness of my tent, I could feel its magnetic pull. By 4:00 A.M., my body was full of food and coffee, eager to hit the trail. Seeing a faint glow of light from the tent of my friend "Disco," I walked over to him and whispered, "Hey Disco, it's Christmas morning." We couldn't stop smiling. This was the day we had been waiting for - after five months of swollen feet, sweat, and pain, the end was near.

The hike up Katahdin was spectacular with lots of hand-over-hand climbing, bouldering and a vertical ascent of 4,000 feet in five miles. The last few steps were effortless as I glided to the top. The wooden sign at the top spoke of a little mountain in Georgia some 2,160 miles away. We had done it! I glanced over at Disco who was sitting in the rocks, and choking back tears, in his slow southern drawl he said, "It's beautiful, Grubby. It's just beautiful . . ."

And it was.

We sat there for a long time drinking in the moment - savoring it. Surrounded by nature in all of her glory: lakes, mountains, and forests stretched out as far as the eye could see. Words need not be spoken.

A few days earlier, Disco had received a package in the mail containing the ashes of his friend "Gator-Boy," who had died suddenly while thru-hiking in 1997. I couldn't help but wonder who this man was that had shared the same dream as me, and only in his early twenties, what a shame his life had been taken at such a young age. I wished I had known him, but somehow I knew that I already did. It was a solemn reminder of how fortunate I was to be standing on top of this mighty mountain: happy, healthy, and full of life. How fortunate I was that in one of my 28 falls I did not twist an ankle or blow out a knee. How fortunate I was to live my dream.

After a moment of silence, Disco cast the ashes into the air. They hung for a moment, and with a gust of wind, they were gone.

6

The Bears of Yosemite

Within national parks in the United States, your best chance of encountering a black bear at close range is in Yosemite. Yosemite has more "problem bears" within its boundaries than any other piece of public land in the lower 48. I would learn this first-hand during the summer of 2002.

I had planned a hike of the famed 211-mile John Muir Trail (JMT) with a friend from an old Forest Service job and another friend from grad school. We had made the usual preparations for how far we would hike each day and how much food we would need to carry. The one missing piece in my planning was how to deal with black bear encounters, which I had been told were inevitable on the JMT. I was in the Virginia Tech Outdoor Club at the time and knew that one of our members had hiked the JMT the previous summer. She agreed to meet me for a coffee to talk trail.

"Are you carrying a bear canister?" she asked me right off the bat.

"Wasn't planning to," I offered.

Bear canisters are hard-sided cylinders that backpackers can carry to protect their food. They are bulky, heavy and can be quite expensive for someone on a budget like me. And the worst part is that most of them won't hold more than a couple of days of food.

She gave me a questioning look and proceeded to let me know what that decision could mean in no uncertain terms.

"What are you going to do when a bear comes into your camp at night looking for food?" she asked.

The way she had phrased the question definitely caught my attention. Essentially it wasn't a matter of if but when.

"I'm going to bang some pots and make that sound a house cat makes when it sees a bird outside the kitchen window," I replied. "There will be three of us anyway and we aren't planning to camp in established campsites or cook where we camp."

The theory amongst some hiking "experts" was that black bears, especially protected national park black bears, were opportunists. They figured out a long time ago that humans camped in the same spots every night and they cooked where they camped. If you wanted to avoid bears, it was just a matter of not cooking where you camped or camping where other people cooked.

Meg bought into this theory wholeheartedly and relaxed a little bit after she understood that I understood that bears were opportunists that make their nightly rounds at the same campsites every night. She said those were all good things and that if we were willing to risk not carrying bear canisters, we'd need to follow our strategy to a tee.

She also told me to expect being asked by the folks at the backcountry permit office if we had bear canisters. The correct answer was "yes."

***

After a red-eye flight from Alabama to California, Mike and I got picked up by Kate in downtown Sacramento. With great anticipation, we headed east out of town towards the lofty granite mountains of Yosemite. The plan was to hit the permit office early the next morning and be in line once the doors opened. We weren't the only group with that same idea and ended up waiting in a long line of folks eager to get permits, many of whom had their bear canisters in hand to proudly display to the permit person.

My stomach sank a bit. Although bear canisters were not legally required in the early 2000's at Yosemite (they are now), they were HIGHLY encouraged. In other words, you'd need a permission slip from the head of the National Park Service himself in order to get a backcountry permit in Yosemite without a bear canister. Going through Yosemite without a permit would result in a $100 fine if caught.

"How may I help you today?"

"We are hiking the John Muir Trail and would like to get a backcountry permit," I replied, smiling.

"Do you have bear canisters or would you like to rent them?" she asked.

It was literally the first question out of her mouth. I couldn't believe it.

"Yes we do and they are already packed up," I replied without hesitation. I had to tell her something – I figured that she wouldn't have been to sympathetic to our excuse about not being able to afford them and not wanting to add the additional three pounds that they weigh to our already heavy packs.

"Great. How many nights do you plan to camp while on the JMT?"

I was shocked. It was too easy. I had just blatantly lied through my teeth but apparently had done it with enough confidence that I got no follow up questions about the bear canisters. I wasn't asked to produce them or prove in any way, shape or form that we had them with us. Mind-boggling, really. This was a stroke of luck because if I had been pressed, I had no Plan B, since Plan A had only recently been concocted, and I would have been forced to get down on my knees and beg forgiveness.

"We're planning on 17 nights, starting in Yosemite Valley today," I offered.

"All the campsites in Yosemite Valley are booked up for the next 2 days. Today is Thursday. I can get you a reservation for Saturday night," she explained.

I felt like I was at the front desk of a Day's Inn. Saturday night was no good. It was Thursday morning and we were ready to hit the trail. Today! The last thing we wanted to do was twiddle our thumbs for the next 48 hours when we could be out there in the high country laying down miles.

"Are there any other options for hiking out today and camping tonight?" I asked.

"Not for Yosemite Valley but there is for here. You can hike out of Tuolumne Meadows and camp near the Lyell Creek Bridge."

"Great. We'll take it," I said without hesitation.

"I need you to fill out this form stating how many nights you will be camping in each jurisdiction," she told me as she handed me a sheet of paper.

"Ok." I offered. I got into the routine of saying "Ok" or "Yes" to every question she asked me regardless of the true answer. I knew that she had a set list of questions she had to ask everyone requesting a permit. I also knew that if she was given any answer other than the "correct" answer, there would be trouble. And frankly I just wanted to hit the trail. My brain was fried after having just finished my Master's thesis defense at Virginia Tech two weeks prior. I would have told the permit lady anything she wanted to hear if it could have gotten us out the door more quickly.

The piece of paper she handed me had the following names down the left side of the sheet: Yosemite National Park, Minarets Wilderness, Devils Postpile National Monument, John Muir Wilderness and Sequoia/Kings Canyon National Park.

I had absolutely no clue which jurisdiction we would be camping in during the course of a 2 ½ week John Muir Trail hike, except that I figured we'd camp at the Lyell Creek Bridge tonight since that is what our permit said we had to do. As far as the sixteen other nights on the JMT, I had no idea. All I knew is that we needed to hike 13 miles per day to do the trail in 17 days and that was as far as any of us had thought it through. And in regards to the "jurisdiction" we would be camping in on specific nights, I could barely spell jurisdiction much less know which one we'd be in.

So instead, I treated it like a Sudoku puzzle and penciled in numbers that added up to seventeen.

"Great. Looks good," she told me after analyzing my answers.

"Now I just need you to sign this permit and you'll be on your way."

I signed the permit and asked how much the permit would cost.

"They're free. There's no charge. Have a great hike," she said without skipping a beat as she glanced over my shoulder to the next person in line.

I walked over to Kate and Mike a bit amused and slightly dumbfounded by the conversation I just had. All that rigmarole just to get a free piece of paper that I was legally required to attach to my pack in order to camp in the woods. You gotta love the National Park Service.

***

The permit we were able to get had us hiking south out of the backcountry permit station into Lyell Meadows along the John

Muir Trail. That would mean skipping the first 24 miles between Yosemite Valley and Tuolumne Meadows. We discussed a few options including taking a chance on hiking out of Yosemite Valley, but cooler heads prevailed. We decided that we were already risking it by not having bear canisters so we should at least camp where the permit said we were supposed to camp on the first night. We pledged to come back and hike those 24 miles after we had finished up the long walk from the permit station to Mt. Whitney, the JMT's southern terminus.

We locked up Kate's car, hoisted our packs and headed out without delay. It was great to finally be walking on a dirt path ... done with my Master's, done with the trail prep and done with the permit lady. We were on trail, permit in hand and nothing could stop us now!

And due to our permit, we were only allowed to hike six miles that first day through Lyell Meadows to camp near Lyell Creek. We made quick work of those six miles and arrived at Lyell Creek to find many different groups of people camping in a variety of established campsites. There were Boy Scout troops, couples, families, groups of five, groups of 10 and a few others all mixed about. Everyone appeared to have bear canisters, that is, everyone but us.

Hmm. So the plan was not to cook where we were going to camp and not to camp in established campsites. Tonight we would be cooking where we were camping and camping in an established campsite. Not good. But I thought to myself, what really were the chances of having a bear come into our campsite? I mean, come on. I had hiked the entire 2,200-mile Appalachian Trail in 1999 and never had a bear come into my camp at night and on the AT, I cooked where I camped and camped in established sites almost nightly for five months.

Just to play it "safe," we decided to cook at the bridge over Lyell Creek and camp a hundred yards or so away. Never mind that we were surrounded by a gob of people that were cooking right in their campsites. The smell of campfires and camp food had already been wafting in the air for an hour or two.

We made quick work of dinner and proceeded to set up camp. Mike and I each had our own tents and Kate was using one of those blue tarps onto which you normally rake leaves for her shelter. Personally, I was glad to be zipped up in my light-weight tent and not under a wide-open tarp. After all, I didn't want bugs crawling all over me or heaven forbid, bears sniffing around me.

We spent about 30 minutes methodically hanging our food bags over a tree branch near our tents. The "counterbalance method" as it is called (not allowed anymore due to its high rate of failure) was our chosen technique of bear thwarting. It works like this. You tie a rock onto the end of a rope. Then you throw the rock with attached rope over a branch. Now you pull the rock-end of the rope back up to the branch and attach a food bag to the other end in your hand. Next you push the food bag up in the air until the rock end comes down. You grab the rock (with rope still attached) and hoist the food bag end up to the branch. Take the rock off and attach another food bag essentially creating a counter weight. Push the second set of food bag(s) up towards the branch and the other food bag comes down. Voila . . . you have just counterbalanced a set of food bags. Clear as mud eh?

The key is to make sure the food bags are a couple feet above your head well off the ground and ten or so feet out from the trunk of the tree. At least that's what all the hiking guide-books say to do.

After sitting around and chattering for a bit about how great we counterbalanced our food and about anything and everything except bears (and bear canisters or a lack thereof), darkness moved in and it was time to hit the hay. We all decided to put a small pile of rocks right in front of our tent doors . . . just in case we needed them to fend off any midnight marauders (a last minute tip Meg had given me).

I was really looking forward to getting some rest as I had logged only six hours of sleep the past two nights due to the mêlée of packing and repacking and double-checking and flying to Sacramento. I hustled into my tent, organized a few things, crawled in my bag and zipped it up. At last, I was safe in my tent and snug in my bag. Happy that the day was over and glad we had started the hike, I lay dozing for about 20 minutes on the verge of a good night's sleep.

"BEAR!" Kate screamed at the top of her lungs! "BEAR, BEAR, BEAR!"

"Oh shit!" I exclaimed as I grabbed my headlamp while simultaneously fumbling with the zipper of my sleeping bag. I had literally been in my tent only a half hour before the first bear showed up.

"Mike, get the hell out here. There's a bear!" I yelled after realizing he was fast asleep and had not heard any of the commotion.

Kate was already in food bag defense mode and had hurled half a dozen rocks at the beast. I followed suit. We hollered and threw rocks and the bear ambled unhurriedly around the edge of our campsite as it made its way to the next campsite. Every five minutes we heard a different group of people yelling and banging pots as the bear made its rounds to each and every campsite in the vicinity of Lyell Creek bridge.

Mike finally made it out of his tent to ask what was going on.

"Was it a bear?" he stammered.

"Yes it was a bear and what the hell took you so long?" Kate asked.

"I guess I was asleep."

"Dude, you gotta be ready to go. If these bastards take our food, we're screwed," I piped in as rationale to take less than 20 minutes to get out of one's tent when a 300 lb. bear is 15' away.

Besides the rush of adrenaline and panic, I had this sinking feeling in my stomach. Here we were not even a half day into a two-and-a-half week hike, void of bear canisters and already besieged by bears. Was it going to be like this every night on the JMT? Maybe we should have brought bear canisters, I thought to myself? Should we hike back to the permit station and rent canisters?

I shined my headlamp down at my watch: 10:20 P.M. Good grief. First light wasn't until 6:00 A.M. or so. It was going to be a long night.

We restacked our individual rock piles by our shelters, crawled back into our sleeping bags and tried to call it a night . . . again. Periodically I would hear the distant screams of panicked campers attempting to scare a 300-pound bear out of their campsite. I closed my eyes again and started to drift off to sleep.

"BEAR!" Kate screamed at the top of her lungs again! "BEAR, BEAR, BEAR!"

This time both Mike and I were up and out of our tents within 60 seconds, headlamps ablaze as the fat bear came scampering back down the tree from which we had counterbalanced our food bags. We shouted and screamed and threw rocks and the bear headed out of our camp once again.

"Alright. We've gotta come up with a Plan B. This bear is just making the rounds. It's gonna come back," I predicted.

I had barely finished my sentence before we heard high-pitched shrieks from the campsite on the other side of the ravine from us.

"Yeah, let's roll," Mike suggested with a bit of urgency in his voice.

With that we hurriedly took down our tents and packed up our gear. We wanted to get out of there before the bruin came back. We took our food bags down from the tree, threw them in our packs and hiked out. My watch said it was 11:30 P.M.

We decided we should hike for at least one hour before setting up our second camp in order to put enough distance between the bear and ourselves. We could likely cover two miles an hour in the dark, I calculated.

The trail led higher into Upper Lyell Canyon, an area strewn with rocks, talus slopes and void of much in the way of flat camping.

Kate spotted a reasonably horizontal ledge upon which she could pitch her tarp. Now it was close to 1:00 A.M. and frankly I would have camped on a bed of nails if it meant bear-free sleep. We lined up in our sleeping bags under her tarp like sardines in a can after piling a large cache of small rocks on either side to throw at the next bear that showed up. Ironically, I was glad to be smushed in with Mike and Kate under the exposed blue tarp that I had shunned as inferior just a few hours earlier. We would be much more efficient at mounting a bear counterattack when camped in such close quarters.

I lay awake for hours. Every gust of wind, snap of a twig, and a host of likely imagined noises amplified in my mind and meant only one thing - another bear. I'd look up and see nothing as I peered out from under Kate's tarp. I think I finally drifted off to sleep around 4:00 A.M. with visions of bears dancing in my head. Welcome to the JMT.

***

Our hike on the JMT from there to Mt. Whitney went off without any troubles. We encountered no other bears in the night and stuck to our plan of not camping in established campsites and not cooking where we camped. Typically we would stop around four o'clock or so every day to cook our evening meal and then we'd hike at least an hour or two before setting up camp for the night off trail in a random spot. Some nights we were perched on rocky cliffs, others in a quiet stand of Jeffrey pines and some in breezy green meadows full of tall grasses complete with the songs of hundreds of unseen birds.

The day we hiked by Rae Lakes we ran into a lady who shared a tale of woe with us. She had been camping at Rae Lakes the previous summer and had placed her bear canister full of food about ten feet in front of her tent. She had her permits and had basically done everything "correctly," according to Park Service regulations. At some point in the night, a bear came into her campsite, spied the bear canister in front of her tent and took off with it. She opted not to give chase to the bear given that it was 3:00 A.M., pitch dark, she was by herself and he was a bear. I can't say that I blame her. The following morning she spent the better part of four hours scouring the area around her campsite. No sign of her bear canister or the bear. She had done everything "right" and lost all of her food in the process. Luckily for her, she was able to scrounge enough food off other backpackers to make it back out to the trailhead where she had parked her car. This marked the first time on the JMT that I actually felt we might have possibly made the right decision by not carrying bear canisters!

After summiting Mt. Whitney, the highest point in the lower 48 at 14,491 feet, we hitched a series of rides back to Tuolumne Meadows. True to our promise, we decided to hike the 24 miles from Tuolumne Meadows to Yosemite Valley. After all, we were here to hike the entire JMT and that 24 miles is all that separated us from completing the length of the trail.

The thought of going back into the permit station to talk to the permit lady in order to get a backcountry permit for our

24-mile hike was more than any of the three of us could stomach. Besides, we were only going to be camping for one night. We'd hike 17 or so miles tomorrow, camp, and then hike six down to Yosemite Valley after bagging Half Dome along the way. No big deal. We'd stealth camp out of sight of any rangers and all bears and everything would be fine as muscadine wine.

The plan was hatched and we spent the night hoisting a few cold ones at a pay campground near Tuolumne Meadows, enjoying a well-deserved night's rest. We felt confident that our bear troubles were over and that we'd have the JMT in the bag real soon. What we took for granted, though, was that we were back in the black bear epicenter of the United States: Yosemite National Park.

Two hours into the hike the next morning, Mike decided he just didn't care about those last 24 miles. Frankly I didn't either but decided, along with Kate, to keep going just to keep going. Mike grabbed the car key from Kate and backtracked five or so miles to the parking lot. Kate and I pressed on. It was mostly downhill and the end was in sight, plus we were going to get a shot at the famed Half Dome on our way into Yosemite Valley. It would be worth it, I told myself.

Around five o'clock we stopped and cooked dinner. We had already done 16 of the 17 miles we'd planned to do that day and realistically could have kept going and finished the entire 24 by dark. But that wasn't the plan and if we did that, we'd miss the hike up Half Dome.

We had literally just packed up from dinner when a backcountry ranger came walking towards us on the trail.

"Hello. Can I see your permit?" she asked.

With no time to think I said, "We're not camping tonight. We're hiking all the way into Yosemite Valley."

The ranger glanced at her watch and said, "You know Yosemite Valley is about eight miles from here?"

"Sure do. And we've got four hours before it gets dark. We'll make it, no problem," I stated confidently.

"Sounds good. Have a nice hike," the ranger said and moved on.

Kate and I walked for about five minutes before saying a word to each other.

"That was a close call. Nice work," she commented.

"All I want to do is finish this damn trail and I'll tell a ranger anything they want to hear if it means finishing without having to fork out $100 in fines," I stated.

We hiked on for a few more minutes and then spotted a flat outcropping above the trail and somewhat out of view of any rangers or people that would happen by. We both looked around to make sure that our ranger wasn't walking back towards us and then bolted up the hill and out of sight. We found a nice flat camping area on a bed of soft pine needles. It was warmer than most nights due to the low elevation at which we were camping on our descent to Yosemite Valley. And we estimated that we were less than a mile away from the Half Dome turnoff. This had worked out just perfectly.

Kate and I decided that we would both camp under her blue tarp. We'd be able to break camp more quickly in the morning to get an early start up Half Dome before the crowds showed up. The downside to camping under an open tarp on a warm night is that the bugs could be a problem if they were out. Large black ants were all over the place but I didn't think it'd be a big deal. Once it got dark, I called it a day and climbed into my sleeping bag. Roughly every 15 minutes for the next few hours I would wake up to a large black ant biting my neck or chest after having crawled into my sleeping bag with me. It became so frequent that I stopped unzipping my bag to throw them out; instead I just started squashing them through my shirt with my thumb and left their carcasses underneath. I'd empty them all out in the morning.

It had been almost a full thirty minutes since my last ant bite and I had almost drifted off to sleep. Kate and I both bolted upright after hearing the scampering of an animal up the tree directly beside us . . . the tree in which we had chosen to counterbalance our food bags. We grabbed our headlamps to find that only mine was working. I shined it up the tree above our tarp to find two bear cubs scampering out on the limb where our food bags were suspended. "Son of a bitch," I mumbled in disbelief.

We started yelling and throwing rocks from our trusty pile that we had built before going to sleep. My immediate thought is "where's momma bear?" Typically cubs don't stray far from their mothers. Both cubs came bolting down the tree and took off into the woods.

"Kate, you and I both know that they are going to be back. They know we are here and they know we have food," I stated emphatically.

A glance at my watch told me it was 1:45 A.M. Geez Louise. Before I could even look up the two cubs were back. We really lit into them this time, yelling curses and screaming bloody murder. I may have even made a few of those cat noises.

"Let's go," Kate said without a second thought.

We packed up our gear, got the food bags out of the tree, stuffed them in our packs and hiked out. The whole process took less than ten minutes this time.

Within five minutes the batteries on my headlamp died. Crap. There is nothing quite like fumbling around for spare batteries in the darkness of unfamiliar woods with two bear cubs and likely a momma bear in the vicinity with no light due to dead batteries. Kate found a butane lighter in her pack which provided enough light for me to find my spare set of batteries.

After getting my headlamp back up and running again, we hiked out. Since Kate had no working headlamp or flashlight of any kind, she walked close behind me while I shined the light down on my feet. That way she could see where I was walking and technically I could see where I was stepping; however, I could not see the trail ahead very well. More than once we lost the dirt path and had to scurry around to find it. We had already passed the junction to the Half Dome trail and wrote off this side trip as a casualty of our latest bear encounter. Half Dome would have to wait for another day.

At 4:00 A.M. we arrived at the Little Yosemite Valley Camping area after two hours of hiking. There were tents set up everywhere and metal bear boxes galore. I was ecstatic to find a metal bear box that would keep all our food secure from any bears that tried to get it. Kate and I found a flat spot to lay the tarp on the ground. We opened the bear box to toss in our food and its creaky hinges woke up a nearby camper.

"Who's out there," a voice from a nearby tent nervously questioned?

"There's just two of us. We got in late and we're just putting our food in the bear box," I replied. "Sorry to wake you.

"Phew," he grunted. "I was worried you all were the bear that's been in the campground the last four hours. People have been screaming all night," he stated with relief.

That's just great news, I thought to myself. It's 4:00 A.M. and all we want to do is sleep and there's a different bear in this area that has caused people to scream all night. That's just super.

Kate and I crawled into our sleeping bags after deciding we'd have to break camp and head out before the sun came up since we didn't have a permit and ran the risk of getting caught by a ranger. So we took a two-hour nap, packed up again and hiked out around 6:00 A.M. I was somewhere between sleep-deprived delirium and feeling as though I had just been injected with a horse tranquilizer as we stepped back out onto the trail.

After less than an hour, we ran into Mike, heading up the trail towards us. Apparently he had a bear encounter in the wee hours of the night also. Mike had gone back to the car at Tuolumne Meadows and driven down to Yosemite Valley. All the pay campgrounds were full so he decided to park the car and hike up the JMT with the intention of joining us for the jaunt up Half Dome the following morning. He didn't have a backcountry permit for camping that night either so he headed off the trail to camp in an out-of-view spot.

At 3:00 A.M. a bear showed up and grabbed his backpack, which was lying right beside his tent. He got out and gave the bear chase before reconsidering his situation: It was 3:00 A.M., dark as a dungeon and a large black bear had just taken his backpack and was heading deep into the woods with it. Mike decided to head back to his tent and mark the backpack down as a loss. "You win some, you lose some," he told us.

At first light he went out to search for his backpack, which he actually found. But that's all he found. His camp stove and cook fuel were gone. Luckily for both the bear and Mike, he did not have any food with him. Unluckily for him, however, the stove was brand new and was now gone forever.

After running into each other, we swapped stories as we headed back to Kate's car in Yosemite Valley. We rounded one final bend and popped out in front of a large National Park Service sign that said, "Mt. Whitney – 211 miles." We had just finished the entire length of the John Muir Trail. All I wanted to do was go somewhere – anywhere that didn't involve camping permits, park rangers and sleep-depriving bears.

"Beer is on me," I offered in my concluding remarks after just having finished the famed 211-mile trek. "Now let's get the hell out of here."

7

Zee Vater

The Great Divide Basin is a geographic feature in southern Wyoming where the Continental Divide splits to form east and west rims. It's the only place along the Continental Divide in North America where this happens. The rest of the Divide runs as one continuous land feature that separates water that flows into the Pacific Ocean and water that flows into the Atlantic Ocean.

This one million acre basin is very dry, mostly flat and a world all its own. If you've seen photos from the Mars Rover, you've got a good idea of what "the Basin" looks like. Outside of a tumbleweed rolling by, antelope and scattered oil rigs are about the only sights a Continental Divide Trail (CDT) thru-hiker sees when traversing the 120-mile stretch of trail from South Pass City to Rawlins through the Basin.

Although this section is somewhat featureless and quite hot, the flat terrain gives thru-hikers a good opportunity to lay down some big miles. We had planned to cover the 120-mile distance in 4 days - or 30 miles per day. This was a bit ambitious considering that our previous biggest mile day on the CDT between the Canadian border and South Pass City was a paltry 24 miles. We were going to have to ramp up things a bit to start doing 30's successfully.

P.O.D. and I had grouped up with five other CDT thru-hikers to push through the Basin together. We all figured that the camaraderie would help with the big miles and monotonous terrain. Tradja, Jess, Mags, Skittles and Speedo, in addition to P.O.D. and I, made up our dodgy chain gang. Speedo is a half Finnish / half German guy from Bonn (home of the world's greatest chocolates he assured us) who had come over to the states after four years of planning and preparation to hike the CDT. We met him on the first day of our hike in Glacier National Park where he told us then that he thought he would be hiking by himself the entire way from Canada to Mexico. I could only imagine what he was thinking now as we rolled seven deep into the Basin.

***

To one degree or another, all of us experienced a bit of chafing due to the dry conditions, the hot days and the big miles. Chafing is a skin irritation caused by skin rubbing against skin. The chafing most of us suffered from was on the inner thighs as a result of salty sweat drying on the thighs, which then rubbed together with every step. Compounded over a 12-hour hiking day and a gazillion steps, things had gotten painful for some of us, to say the least.

Hikers have come up with all kinds of remedies to stop chafing, some of which are even listed in hiking guidebooks. Applying diaper rash ointment to the affected area is popular. Some folks still use Vaseline. Others use Bodyglide or Sportslick, which resemble a stick of deodorant. A few hikers I have talked to swear by Astroglide . . . a "personal lubricant." The manliest of hikers have been known to brave drug store clerks for a tube of Vagisil, which apparently also works. There is even a product called "Anti Monkey Butt Powder" marketed towards truck drivers, bicyclists, horseback riders and extreme sports enthusiasts. I don't really consider long-distance hiking an extreme sport in the sense that say BASE jumping or big wave surfing is an extreme sport; however, I do know hikers that in all probability would have paid $100/oz for some Anti Monkey Butt Powder when their chafing became severe. You can tell who's got it too . . . it's the hikers walking with a short step or half step, butt cheeks clinched together, sweat beading down their face. I can tell you from first-hand experience it is excruciatingly painful somewhat like lemon juice and salt being rubbed on an open wound. Pure torture really.

All of us were doing bigger mileage days, which multiplied our chafing problems significantly. Washing up in a stream or river wasn't an option either. The Basin is infamous amongst CDT thru-hikers for its lack of water and foul water sources. Water in the Basin is in a closed system – what rain that does fall stays in the Basin and rain that falls outside the east and west rims of the Continental Divide never makes it into the Basin. What hikers are left with is a number of cattle troughs, man-made reservoirs, and questionable springs, many of which contained an oily sheen on their surface. Every now and again a windmill would appear out of nowhere and if the wind was blowing and the blades were spinning, ice-cold spring water was being pumped out from deep underground. Those windmills were few and far between during this 120-mile segment and they typically weren't marked on any of our maps so we had no way of knowing where they were located.

On our 3rd day in the Basin we reached Brenton Springs, which was a little oasis amongst the sand and sagebrush. The seven of us sat on the soft green grass amongst the willows surrounding the spring to cook dinner and pass around the 12 oz. bottle of a random grape-flavored malt beverage that Mags had found sitting atop a fence post earlier in the day – a bit of "trail magic." Even though it was lukewarm, and a bit dusty, and something I would never consider buying for my own personal consumption back in the civilian world, it tasted fantastic and I would have happily had a six-pack to myself if six had been available.

It was still light out when we finished our evening meal and about half of us decided to push on. It was roughly seven miles to the next water source, which apparently consisted of a 60-gallon metal drum with a faucet that had been installed by a local rancher - at least that's what the water info on our maps said. P.O.D. and I set out first with Speedo and Skittles about 30 minutes behind. The light went from dusk to non-existent in about an hour, which made navigating a bit tricky. I've always said that when the lights go out on the CDT, all bets are off. The CDT is so poorly marked in places that it is a chore to navigate in broad daylight let alone the dark of night.

An hour later we hiked into the area containing the metal drum supposedly spouting fresh, clear, cold water . . . our final destination for the night. Unfortunately we couldn't find it. We scouted around for 15 minutes and that drum was nowhere to be found; it was just too dark to locate anything. I had flash-backs to Yellowstone as our GPS unit was telling us we were standing right on top of the drum with the faucet; however, the only water we could find consisted of some shallow trickles of brown liquid amongst a sea of cow pies intermittently flowing down the edge of an abandoned dirt road. We surmised the water was originating from the drum but following those trickles only led to dead ends. We resigned ourselves to set up our tent and call it a night. The water would be there in the morning and we would actually be able to see the drum without the aid of a headlamp. And anyway, we didn't really need the water as we had already cooked dinner.

The wind had picked up dramatically in the previous hour and setting up our tent became a two-person effort. P.O.D. would stand and hold down one side of our tent while I would stake down the other. Blowing sand compounded our problems and forced us to turn our heads to one side as we blindly staked the thing down. The tent was being whipped about like a rag doll in a tornado and it took us a solid 20 minutes just to get it secured to the ground.

Right about that time, Skittles and Speedo showed up. We saw their headlamps beaming through the dark about 10 minutes before we could make out their silhouettes.

Speedo scurried up to us and in his thick German accent asked, "Vair is zee vater?" with a bit of urgency.

I replied, "Man, we just spent 20 minutes looking for it. We couldn't find it but it's definitely nearby. We're going to wait until the morning. It'll be easier to locate then."

"I must find zee vater," Speedo proclaimed and immediately took off to find the metal drum.

Skittles set up his tent with a bit of effort in the gale force winds and blowing sand. Every now and then I'd peer out into the inky black night from the door of our tent and see Speedo's headlamp bobbing around in search of the "zee vater." I shook my head knowing that it would be next to impossible to find the metal drum given how dark, dusty and windy it was.

Thirty minutes later Speedo came back to camp defeated, not having found "zee vater."

"Hey Speedo, I've got a little bit of water you can have until morning if you need it," P.O.D. offered.

Speedo replied, "I need a lot of vater and I need it now."

P.O.D. retorted, "I don't have much water but you are welcome to take a ¼ liter or so. What do you need it for anyway?"

"I have this schayfing."

"You mean chafing?"

"Yes, schayfing," Speedo replied.

P.O.D. asked, "Where is the chafing?"

Speedo got a bewildered grin on his face and stated, "I can't remember the name of the place Chong (another CDT hiker) told me. It is between my nutzack and my azzhole."

We almost fell over laughing and I offered to Speedo that this place has many names in the English language: "chode, sandbar, grundle, taint, durf, perineum, coronal ridge, nacho."

American slang can be an odd concept to foreigners. I was once given a quizzical look by a different German hiker on the PCT in 2004 after answering her question on what a "durf" was. She told me that in Germany they didn't have names for "these things" and wanted to know why Americans did. I shrugged my shoulders and offered that we wanted to be better than the Germans at something.

Speedo interrupted, "Durf, yes durf. This is the name Chong called it. I need to shave my durf because of the schayfing."

We howled with laughter again and could barely say a word. Skittles was lying on the ground holding his sides, laughing so hard he was crying.

"I must wash the salt crystals out of the hair and shave the durf tonight!" Speedo declared as though the durf was a separate entity not attached to his body.

"I have wet wipes," P.O.D. said with tears of laughter streaming down her face.

"No, I must shave it," Speedo said with unwavering determination.

What happened next is something that will likely be embossed in my memory for the rest of my life. Speedo walked about 10 feet away from our tents, laid out his ground pad, pulled down his pants and inclined his legs into the air. I couldn't look but apparently he extracted his dry razor and - with no water - he shaved his durf in gale force winds in the middle of the night in the Great Divide Basin.

Speedo was an engineer by education and profession and I could only imagine how proud his parents would have been if they could have seen him with his dry razor. Just the thought of this made P.O.D. and I randomly burst into laughing fits for the next hour or so.

"Hey Speedo, how's the razor burn?" I asked through the ongoing sandstorm.

"It's fine, guy. I will be ready to hike another thirty tomorrow morning."

The next morning we all got up at first light and could see the metal drum some 30 yards away from camp. It's funny how it was so close and we knew it was so close yet no one could find it in the darkness. One by one we got in line and filled our water bottles with the clear, cold spring water that was coming out of this defunct rusty metal drum via a spigot. I found myself amazed time and again on the CDT at how mangy a water source could look and how clear the water ended up being once it made its way into my bottle.

About once every hour, someone would rib Speedo a bit about dry shaving his durf and ask him if the chafing was gone. Every time he replied that his expert shaving job saved his life and that he was having no problems today. I don't know if I really believed him, but I do know that he wanted all of us to think that it worked.

By the time we all got into Rawlins the next day, we were grubby and our clothes were filthy due to four long days of pushing big miles thru the Basin. Sandstorms and thirty-mile days have a way of doing that to clothes. After combing the town for about two hours and being turned away from full motel after full motel (due to the boom of oil & gas field workers that had taken the bulk of the lodging), we finally found ourselves bunked in two side by side rooms at the La Bella Motel on the west end of town.

The La Bella is the kind of place that wouldn't be found in *Frommer's* to be rated five-star, or found at all in *Frommer's*, but it was more than adequate for seven dirty hikers. We all desperately needed a shower and laundry and the La Bella had both.

Being the gentleman that he is, Speedo let P.O.D. have first dibbs on a shower since she was a she. I wasn't present for what happened next but Speedo has never denied the accuracy of P.O.D.'s story.

When P.O.D. got out of the shower, towel wrapped around her head, she found Speedo at the bathroom sink working profusely at something. She peered over his shoulder and saw him scrubbing a razor that was caked in hair, dirt and salt.

"Speedo, what are you doing? Is that the razor you used to shave your durf the other night?"

"Yes it is. So what?"

"Is that your toothbrush?"

"Sure. I'll just wash it out with soap after I'm finished."

"No No No! That's gross! Are you crazy?"

Speedo looked at her curiously and after a short pause he said, "What . . . you do not trust zee American soap?"

"No, it's not about the soap. Toothbrushes are cheap. You can't possibly put that toothbrush back in your mouth after you've used it to scrub the salt and durf hairs out of your razor!"

We were all summoned to the bathroom sink and tried desperately for 15 minutes to persuade Speedo to throw away his toothbrush and fork out $2 on a new one.

I'm convinced that Speedo believed in his heart of hearts that we didn't have faith in our own country's soap and that brushing his teeth with a toothbrush that had been used to clean the dirtiest of dirty razors was perfectly acceptable. My only real hope is that his chafing remedy never gets listed in any hiking guidebooks. The last thing we need is a bunch of grubby thru-hikers walking America's longest trails and nicking themselves while dry shaving their most private of privates!

Speedo purchased a new toothbrush three weeks later in Colorado.

8

Waist Deep in Kerrick Creek

The *Pacific Crest Trail Data Book* published by Wilderness Press is a small nondescript book full of numbers. It would look like gobbledygook to the average Joe who opened its pages to see what's inside, but to Pacific Crest Trail thru-hikers, it's the most important bit of information they will carry while walking from Mexico to Canada.

It contains a myriad of information in the form of numeric data points. Each data point contains a landmark name, available amenities (if any), water sources present (if any), mileage, corresponding maps and elevation among other things. There are 84 pages of data points covering the entire 2,663-mile trail. That's a lot of data points.

Although I think it's insane to walk a 2,663-mile trail without a map, more than a few hikers have completed their hikes from Mexico to Canada with just the *PCT Data Book*. Most hikers do carry maps and a guidebook or two. And even amongst the ones who skimp on navigational aids, you would be hard pressed to find a PCT thru-hiker sans *Data Book*.

And though the bulk of hikers have this book in their possession for the five months they are hiking the PCT, not much attention is paid to page five. The title of page five reads: California Snow Depth Measurements. The subtitle reads: *Crossing the High Sierra*. The following statement is laid out:

The High Sierra in California has always been the major barrier for doing a thru-hike of the PCT. If you intend to do a thru-hike, the following equation is provided as a simple way of estimating when to reach Kennedy Meadows, the beginning of the High Sierra, en route to crossing the Sierra. You will still encounter plenty of snow, but it should not be overwhelming.

Kennedy Meadows Day = June 1 + (snow depth at Bighorn Plateau on April 1st divided by 3.5) days

I logged onto the California Department of Water Resources web page to find out what the snow depth was for Bighorn Plateau. It's not very clear from their website, but apparently the California Department of Water Resources (CDWR) is the state outfit in charge of the management and regulation of California's water usage. Water usage is different from year to year in California. If there has been a lot of snow in the high mountains, there will be a lot of snowmelt and water feeding into the rivers later in the summer. The public utilities in California can then predict that a higher percentage of their electric energy generation will come from hydropower in a high snow year and lower percentage in a low snow year. All kinds of other groups and folks use the snow depth data, from agricultural interests, to flood control projects, to local municipalities to fisheries biologists . . . and PCT thru-hikers.

Given the importance and implications of snow amounts in the high mountains, the CDWR has taken such a keen interest in the amount of snow the state receives that it has designated 300 different locations throughout California at which snow depth is measured. Each location, or "snow course," is given a name and number and is measured either manually or electronically every month.

As I sat in the cozy living room of my apartment sipping a hot cup of chai, I clicked over to the California Snow Survey page on my web browser to find the snow depth for April 1st, 2008, at Snow Course #250 (Bighorn Plateau) read 41 inches on the nose. Plugging that into the above equation, I came up with June 13th. So, according to page five of the *Data Book*, if we reached Kennedy Meadows, some 700 miles into our upcoming thru-hike, on June 13th or later, apparently we would likely encounter plenty of snow, "but it should not be overwhelming." I couldn't help but wonder exactly what "overwhelming" meant?

***

On May 31st, we hiked into Kennedy Meadows two full weeks before our pre-calculated "Kennedy Meadows Day" of June 13th. We had made incredible time covering the first 700 miles in 37 days and now we were faced with the repercussions of having gotten there so quickly. Thoughts of "overwhelming snow" resurfaced in my brain as I sat on the porch of the Kennedy Meadows General Store looking out towards the distant mountains.

Strangely enough, we had noticed a smoke plume north of Kennedy Meadows on our hike into the store. After asking around a bit, we were told that the PCT heading north out of Kennedy Meadows was closed due to a wildfire. It reopened back near Trail Pass, some 42 miles north of Kennedy Meadows. What to do?

There were already ten or so hikers at Kennedy Meadows who had arrived the day before. In addition to P.O.D. and myself, hikers continued to show up throughout the day. We decided to take the next day off to recoup from the 700 miles we had just hiked and to plan our strategy for hiking through the High Sierra. Even more hikers showed up the following day and by the time the sun set, there were 25 hikers bottlenecked at Kennedy Meadows . . . and everybody was talking about the fire.

Kennedy Meadows is not really a meadow at all in the sense that you'd think of a big open meadow full of wildflowers and butterflies. There are a few big ranches and houses there, but mostly it is a collection of people who live in trailers. Not like a trailer park, no, more just an assembly of self-sufficient and individualistic people and their eclectic trailers. And there is a store with camp food, snacks, sodas, beer, ice cream and an enormous wraparound porch with a grill that serves burgers. This is the perfect place for PCT hikers to take a day off, because there is nothing to do but sit in the shade and relax. There's also a yippee wiener dog named George that will bite your hand off if you try to pet it but that's neither here nor there.

The talk of the fire ranged from "that fire ain't shit" to "Kennedy Meadows might have to be evacuated." It's funny how rumors and misinformation fly when there's no one who really knows what's going on. To further complicate matters, it was the weekend, which meant that there was no chance in hell we'd be seeing anyone from the Forest Service unless imminent death from a raging inferno overrunning Kennedy Meadows started to become a possibility.

Hikers were plotting and planning as hikers do when they are not upright and walking. A group formed that decided they would hike out the next day and bushwhack around the fire to rejoin the PCT further up. They surmised that if they saw any fire crews or Forest Service folks, they would sneak around them and go unnoticed. Brilliant, I thought to myself. Let's hike into an active wildfire that we have no idea about, sneak around the folks putting out the fire and get burned alive. That sounds like a solid plan.

Not too keen on hiking into a closed section of the PCT with an active wildfire, P.O.D. and I decided that we needed more information in order to make a good decision. We called "Squatch." Squatch was a friend and hiker who we bet would be at home on his computer since he wasn't currently out on the trail. Perhaps he could find some info about the fire on the web.

"Hey Squatch, it's Disco," I blurted out on the receiver of the only pay phone at Kennedy Meadows.

"Hey man. Where are you guys . . . Oregon?" he offered back in jest. He was giving us crap for "hiking too fast" since we had gotten to Kennedy Meadows in May.

"No way, man. We are at Kennedy Meadows and we need your services."

"Swedish massage or pizza delivery?" he fired back.

"I wish. No, we need you to put down that frozen Twinkie (Squatch's favorite) and get us some fire info on the web," I replied. "There's a fire that started a day or two ago just north of Kennedy Meadows and we want to know if there's any info on it and how we can get around it."

Squatch searched around for the next ten minutes and couldn't find much. Even the Forest Service InciWeb site that posts up to the moment info on wildfires all over the country didn't have much to offer - only that the fire had been named the "Clover Fire" and was 0% contained.

Squatch did have maps though. We were flying blind without a good map in front of us (our personal maps showed only a zoomed-in PCT corridor). After much debate and analysis Squatch told us that it looked like our best bet would be to get a ride to Horseshoe Meadows trailhead and hike the two and a half miles on a side trail to rejoin the PCT at Trail Pass.

A quick consultation of our *Data Book* showed us that Trail Pass indeed was about 42 miles north of Kennedy Meadows. That would mean we'd have to skip the closed section of trail and miss 42 miles of the PCT to continue forward unless we were either prepared to A: join the band of genius hikers heading into the fire or B: hang out at Kennedy Meadows for days, weeks, months, infinity, waiting on the fire to be put out and the trail reopened. After a bit of debate and a couple of Coronas, we decided on C: tomorrow morning if we had no legitimate info on the fire from anyone in a forest service or police uniform, we would get ourselves to Trail Pass trailhead and hike on from there. There were a couple of problems with Plan C.

Kennedy Meadows is in the middle of Tuolumne County, California, which is essentially the middle of nowhere. Tuolumne County is over one million acres in size yet is popu- lated by only 54,000 residents. There are shopping malls in Los Angeles that have more people in them.

To get from Kennedy Meadows to Horseshoe Meadows trailhead, one must first get down to Highway 395 via Kennedy Meadows Road. It's a 26-mile drive and the road is mostly windy; the going is slow at best. From 395, it's 55 miles to the hamlet of Lone Pine, a dusty wayside on the east side of the Sierra. And from Lone Pine you've got to find someone willing to drive you 20 miles to Horseshoe Meadows trailhead . . . essentially a parking lot in the middle of the woods.

Monday morning dawned bright and early. It was now June 2nd and we were only a week and a half from our June 13th Kennedy Meadows Day. Perhaps if we just sat around for the next 11 days, the fire would be put out and we could hike out of Kennedy Meadows on the "correct day."

I tried not to think of the snowpack and the term "over- whelming." First things first - before we could confront overwhelming snow, we had to get around the fire. We packed up our camp and headed down to the general store. No one had heard anything about the fire. And the lone toilet that was the only toilet available for public use at Kennedy Meadows had backed up. I saw George the wiener dog. He tried to bite me again. I looked at P.O.D. and we both knew. It was time to go to Horseshoe Meadows trailhead.

I won't go into the details of how we got there. We did get there, however, and it took all day. We had a white-knuckle drive in the back of a truck, hitched a ride in a Wal-Mart 18-wheeler, and received mercy from a local in Lone Pine (a "Lone Pinion") that had seen us thumbing a ride for the better part of four hours up to Horseshoe Meadows.

We set up our tent just before dark at the junction of the PCT and the side trail from Horseshoe Meadows trailhead. We had made it. After hiking only two and half miles, we were utterly exhausted and happy to call it a day. It was June 2nd and we were now two trail days (42 miles) north of Kennedy Meadow. We had essentially rewound the clock to theoretically being two weeks ahead of the June 13th Kennedy Meadows Day that I had calculated some two months ago in my apartment. I had hiked through the High Sierra on the PCT both in 2002 during a John Muir Trail thru-hike and in 2004 during my first PCT hike, but never this early in the season. I didn't really know what to expect - hopefully it would not be overwhelming snow.

One thing became evident rather quickly. We weren't going to be hurting for water. Every creek, stream, river and ounce of water that was flowing was flowing high and fast. In 2004, the snowpack had been 30% below normal for the season and we didn't leave Kennedy Meadows until the second week in June. I had made a game out of seeing how many streams and creeks I could rock hop without getting my feet wet. This year it would be a different story. After only a few hours of hiking the next morning, my feet were already soaked and there was no keeping them dry or rock hopping anything. I still felt that our biggest obstacle in getting through the High Sierra this early would be the snow. I had no idea that it would actually be the streams.

Only a handful of hikers were ahead of us. This meant that we'd not be running into many folks as we made our way across the high passes of the Sierra. Cell phones are virtually useless in the vast Sierra peaks - the first signal I received was some 170 trail miles north of Kennedy Meadows. Knowing that we were not likely to have ready access to help if something went wrong, we took extra caution ascending and descending the snow-covered slopes. And we ascended and descended many snow-covered slopes on our way north over the next two weeks.

After leaving camp that morning, we hiked up to Cottonwood Pass, which isn't much of a pass at all. As a matter of fact, it's the only one of the nine high passes of the Sierra that the PCT does not go up and over. It's more of a trail junction than anything and the PCT skirts to the side of it. One guidebook I remembered reading stated that the snow conditions at Cottonwood Pass would be similar to what a hiker could encounter all the way to Tuolumne Meadows, some 200 miles north. We were walking on dry ground at Cottonwood Pass with only patchy snow nearby; it seemed AOK to me.

Our next high pass would be Forester Pass. At 13,200' in elevation, it is the highest pass in the Sierra and the highest point on the PCT. I felt that it would be a true indicator of how much snow we were up against and how tough it would be through the rest of the Sierra.

We had a virtually snow-free hike up the south face of Forester Pass . . . similar to the conditions in 2004. On our way down the north facing side we had a bit more snow, but that's to be expected on a north-facing slope at 13,000'. It wasn't that difficult although we descended with our ice axes in hand ready to self-arrest if we slipped. About halfway down I turned around to look back at the pass. I could see five other thru-hikers just starting their descent. I knew they were thru-hikers because nobody else in their right minds hikes the High Sierra in early June on purpose.

The spring snow on the ground had melted a bit underneath the surface and we did some post-holing as we finished the descent to Vidette Meadow to camp for the evening. We had a busy campsite as the five hikers we had seen on our descent joined us. We all talked about how easy and straightforward the climb and descent over Forester had been. I went to sleep that night thinking that it was going to be an easy seven or eight days into Reds Meadow, our next real stop.

We were planning to hike straight through without going down to the town of Independence or to Vermillion Valley Resort – frequently used resupply points amongst PCT thru-hikers. Both places were well off trail and would cost us an extra day or so just to get in and out of them. We had also decided that we were willing to trudge a few extra days with really heavy packs full of additional food just to be self-sufficient and void of the ever-present distractions found in trail towns. It would be tough but hopefully rewarding.

Three miles north of our campsite in Vidette Meadow, the Kearsarge Pass trail heads to the east for the town of Independence. The five that had camped with us the night before were all going down to town. We bid them farewell and continued on the PCT. As we hiked up to 11,900' Glen Pass, the snow got deeper than it had been at any point on Forester Pass and we had to stop and check the map to make sure we were headed up the right pass.

The view from Glen was spectacular with high jagged peaks in every direction. We spotted patchy snow and ice blue lakes with large floating bergs in the distance including the series of lakes to which we were headed. In between the lakes and us lay a large steep snowfield 10 football fields in length descending steeply towards a high alpine tarn. I tried to force the knot in my throat back to my stomach, but was a bit intimidated by what lay in front of me.

There was an obvious trail of footprints heading immediately to the right of the pass. P.O.D. and I talked it over and decided that it would take us forever to try and follow the footsteps down the steep snowfield. Instead we would glissade. Glissading is typically done by treating your hiking boots as skis while using your ice axe as a break. It's not easy and we weren't wearing hiking boots. Both of us had on low top trail running shoes. Instead, we planned to glissade the way most thru-hikers do; we would sit on our butts and slide down using the bottom of our ice axes and the heels of our feet as brakes. I was more than a bit nervous about glissading down this slope as I had never descended 2,000' on my butt.

P.O.D. was feeling a little more confident. She walked out about 30 yards from the top of the pass, sat on her butt, positioned her ice axe and released it. Immediately she started to slide but she dug in her ice axe to keep the momentum in check. She slid down about 100 yards and then stood up to walk around some rocks. I followed suit and realized that it was actually fairly safe . . . as safe as sliding on your butt down a snowfield too steep to walk down can be. We slid the rest of the way down Glen Pass until it flattened out. We both commented on how cold our butt cheeks were but otherwise were no worse for the wear.

We went up and over Pinchot Pass the next day using much the same strategy. The going was slow but nothing was overwhelming. Perhaps the *Data Book* was wrong!

We got to the South Fork Kings River to find it wide and pushing – pushing meaning that it was flowing swift enough to push us down! It was midday and the snow high above us was in full sun and melting. Snowmelt feeds down into the rivers and streams below and can turn what is a rock hop in late summer into a class five death trap in early spring. South Fork Kings River got above our knees and it took some careful footing to get from one side to the other without being pushed down by the chilly torrent. As we hiked out of the river from the other side with water gushing out of our shoes, I was a bit perplexed; I hadn't even noticed South Fork Kings River in 2004.

I knew that we had two creeks ahead that might be a problem - Evolution Creek and Bear Creek. Evolution is wider than Bear and if it's pushing, it could definitely present some challenges. When we got to Evolution it was about thigh high at its deepest but the water wasn't moving very swiftly and we made fairly quick work of it. Bear Creek wasn't as wide as Evolution but was pushing a bit. At some point during the thigh-deep crossing my hiking poles started shaking a bit . . . literally vibrating. That's when you know you've got a bit of current to contend with. P.O.D. took her time and also made it across unscathed.

In my mind, we were sitting pretty. We had made it across what I thought were the two toughest fords of the entire Sierra and had already crossed seven of the nine high passes. There were only two more passes left to go and they were lower in elevation than any of the previous passes. No sweat.

Late in the day on June 8th, we reached the trail junction that led down to Lake Edison and Vermillion Valley Resort or

"VVR" as it's known on trail. VVR is a backcountry wayside of sorts, complete with a rustic restaurant, bunkhouse, and a few other amenities. Everything available for sale at VVR has to be trucked in two hours from the nearest town. And because of this, nothing much is cheap. Doing the hike on a budget meant making some sacrifices, so we opted to hike right on by VVR on our way to Reds Meadow and the town of Mammoth Lakes.

We took a quick snack break at the trail junction and decided to push on to get in a few more miles before it got dark. We had about an hour of sunlight left and wanted to get a jump-start on the 3,000' climb to Silver Pass.

About thirty minutes into it, we came to North Fork Mono Creek. Dusk was descending and I hadn't heard anything in particular about Mono Creek so I didn't think twice about charging right in. It was late in the day, and after a full week out there, I was tired and just wanted to get in another mile or so before dark so we could set up camp and call it a day. Halfway across I was in almost waist deep and Mono Creek was really moving. I almost lost my footing and a quick shot of adrenaline surged through my body. Crap. I continued on, making sure that I always had three points of contact on the creek bed as I trudged forward. As soon as I lifted a foot to take a step, the force of the water made my leg flail like a windsock and I had to force my foot down in order not to be completely swept off my feet. To make matters worse, the water through which I was struggling was snowmelt. Snowmelt is cold, really really cold. The longer you are in it, the less feeling you have in your legs. My legs were really starting to ache from the cold just as I made my way onto shore.

I shook myself off and hopped around a bit to get the feeling back into my numb feet. If it's possible to have an ice cream headache in your feet, I had one. I was taken aback at how tough the crossing had been. I turned around and looked at

P.O.D. I had to shout just so she could hear me over the roar of Mono Creek. I told her to take her time and keep three points of contact. She picked up on the concern in my voice and had seen me struggle as I crossed. The look on her face told me that she was a bit worried. She had only one trekking pole to help her cross the stream as she had broken her other one on a nasty descent a few days prior. Neither one of us even considered that grabbing a stick off the ground to substitute for her broken pole would have been a big help.

She started in and right about the point she got thigh deep I could tell she was scared. I would have been scared myself if I hadn't been so dumb. I had convinced myself that this stream crossing wouldn't be a problem and even though it almost swept me off my feet, I was able to cross without the anguish and dread one experiences when crossing a stream they've just seen someone struggle to ford.

As I watched her struggle to the midway point of the stream crossing, I realized how unbelievably brainless we were being. We were crossing a raging river with about 20-30 minutes of daylight left by ourselves in the middle of nowhere with no one to help us if swept downstream. I also realized that I was utterly powerless against the current if P.O.D. went under and got pinned on something. If she did fall, I would literally be watching her drown in front of my eyes and there would be nothing I could do about it. I was starting to freak out but did my best to keep from showing the panic that was now sounding alarm bells throughout my brain. The last thing she needed to see as a hiker struggling to cross a dangerous creek was her hiking partner losing his shit on dry land right in front of her. I kept telling her she was doing great . . . you're almost there . . . just a few more steps . . . three points of contact . . . you're doing awesome.

P.O.D. looked exhausted and somewhat pale as she emerged soaked and shaken from crossing Mono Creek.

"What the hell are we doing out here?" I gushed rhetorically.

"We had no business crossing that stream this late in the day in the condition it was in. If you or I had slipped, we'd be dead, and there would be nothing that either one of us could have done about it. Nothing." I was angry at myself more than anything.

We talked it over briefly and decided to camp at the first flat spot we found. We weren't going to be crossing any more creeks or rivers today, that was for sure. We didn't say much to each other as we set up camp. I think we both realized that we had just rolled the dice and won but could just as easily have lost.

I lay in my sleeping bag wide-eyed going through various scenarios in my head of what could have happened. We were both very lucky and very stupid for crossing Mono Creek this late in the day. We should have camped on the other side of the creek and waited until morning to cross when the water was lower. The water is almost always lower in the early morning as the snowpack up high refreezes a bit overnight and doesn't start melting again until late morning.

Before closing my eyes for good, I pulled out the map to see that we would be crossing Mono Creek two more times and the outlet of Silver Lake once en route to Silver Pass. If we got up early and got a quick start, we could do all these crossings while the water was at it's lowest. I just wasn't sure how low it would be.

Neither of us got much sleep. P.O.D. told me she was awake for two hours thinking about having to ford Mono Creek two more times. We talked over our strategy a bit while packing up our tent. This time we would scout the crossing both up and down from the point where the PCT intersects Mono to see if there was a more shallow spot to cross. And we would find two fat hiking sticks for P.O.D. to use to help her with the ford.

We finished loading our backpacks and ascended in elevation as we made our way up to Mono Creek to cross it again. Upon first glance, the water definitely seemed a bit lower although it was still moving pretty swiftly. But it was not as fast or as deep as the water we had experienced the night before during our first ford of the creek.

We scouted both upstream and downstream to see if there was an easier crossing. There wasn't. We came back to the stream bank after finding a few hiking sticks for P.O.D. to use. I decided to stick with my hiking poles even though they were pretty thin and extremely light.

I uttered, "here goes" in a low voice as I put my right foot into the ice cold water. It was about 6:30 A.M. and the sun had yet to break through the towering pines to warm us. The water temperature made us even colder, but I was glad that it wasn't late afternoon when the water would be really high.

The stream came up to my mid-thigh. That was tolerable. Just as I started to feel a bit of relief, one of my hiking poles disconnected at the middle where it was hinged. The bottom half was apparently wedged between two rocks. I bent down and plunged my arm into the cold waters to try and pry it loose but it wouldn't budge. I was forced to continue crossing the creek without the bottom half of my pole.

I shouted back to P.O.D. that it wasn't nearly as tough as last night. She took her hefty hiking sticks and waded in. With the focus of a samurai, she took one careful step after another, never looking up once, and did the crossing without too much trouble. We both remarked that our feet felt like frozen ice blocks in the few seconds after emerging from the water.

The last ford of Mono Creek and Silver Lake's outlet was cold but not harrowing. It helped that we had done all three early in the day. If it had been mid-afternoon or later, we likely would have had as much trouble as we had the previous night.

The rest of the hike to Tuolumne Meadows went off without too much trouble. We had a few long hours of trying to hike through miles upon miles of "sun cups" heading up and over Island Pass and Donahue Pass. Most important, however, there were no horrific fords.

Heading north out of Tuolumne Meadows, we had about 77 miles to get to Sonora Pass. We would head down from Sonora Pass to the town of Bridgeport, California, for our first real town stop since heading into Mammoth Lakes just after VVR. I perused my *Data Book* and the two guidebooks I was carrying for info on the trail ahead while camped at Tuolumne Meadows.

Most hikers, myself included, also carry the official PCT guidebooks from Wilderness Press and *Yogi's PCT Handbook* from a former PCT thru-hiker named Yogi. The PCT guidebooks give a detailed mile-by-mile description of the actual trail which is really helpful when you're standing at a trail junction and aren't sure which trail is the PCT. Yogi's book gives detailed info on trail towns and quotes from other hikers on various data points . . . including tough fords. I scanned the upcoming section in Yogi's book to see if we had any more fords we needed to be concerned with.

On page 85, I came across the following for Kerrick Canyon Creek: "This was the toughest creek crossing in all three years. VERY strong water."

When she says "toughest creek crossing in all three years," Yogi was saying that it was the toughest ford out of all the fords on the entire 2,663-mile PCT. She had hiked the PCT three times so it wasn't just a fluke; this was the worst of the worst and had been the worst every time she had hiked the trail. Immediately my stomach sank. P.O.D. and I talked about it and tried to play it cool. Essentially we now had 40 miles and two days of hiking in which to agonize over Kerrick Creek. It's kind of like knowing that you have an upcoming root canal appointment and no other choice but to go through with it.

The section of trail from Tuolumne Meadows to Kerrick Creek was tough. Lots of up and down. The trail went up 1,600' and then down 1,000' only to go up again another 1,600'. We were feeling it for sure by the time we descended to Kerrick Canyon.

Kerrick Canyon is reached after a 1,200' descent from Seavey Pass. That descent is all on north-facing ground and there was a lot of remnant snow that had not yet melted even though it was late June. We "shoe-skied" the majority of it, which allowed us to make fairly good time. Shoe-skiing is exactly as it sounds . . . instead of 190cm downhill skis, we skied on the bottom of our low top trail runners!

We were taken aback at what we saw after reaching the banks of Kerrick Creek. The trail stayed on the north side of the creek and the north side was lined with rocky cliffs. North-facing creeksides don't get much sun and are the last areas to become snow-free in the high mountains. In between raging Kerrick Creek and the rocky cliffs where the trail normally resides was a triangular stack of snow about 12' feet high. The top of this 12' foot snow bank resembled a knife-edge. On one side of the knife blade, the snow dropped steeply down straight into the raucous river. On the other side of the blade, it dropped steeply into the rocky cliff. The only options were to either turn back or to walk very very carefully along the knife-edge. There was no room for error.

After going to my mental "happy place" and keeping my ice axe out to self-arrest regardless of which way I fell, the knife edge blunted out and we soon found ourselves on less precarious footing. Three and a half miles later we reached the spot where the PCT crosses Kerrick Creek. Our buddy "Thumbs Up" was already there.

"There's no way to cross it right now. It's too high. I tried three times and had to turn back each time so I'm camping right here on the shore tonight," Thumbs Up told us as we headed down to the crossing to take a look for ourselves.

Thumbs up is about 6' tall and a retired Air Force pilot. He's a tough guy and if he had to turn back three times and set up camp, then we were basically screwed.

Kerrick Creek was a raging torrent. Intimidating, frightening . . . I felt nauseated and faint just looking at it. We scouted both upstream half a mile and downstream half a mile and there was no better place to cross it than where the PCT crosses it. We consulted our maps for another trail crossing of Kerrick Creek somewhere else, anywhere else, but found nothing. Our only hope of getting across it would be to camp and cross early in the morning in hopes that the water level would recede a bit overnight as the snow up high refroze.

Now we had all night to think about how horrible this ford was going to be. As horrible as we may have imagined it, we would later find out that our friend "Stilts" had an experience during his crossing that was much worse than what we would experience.

Stilts, for some reason, was convinced that fording raging streams is best done barefoot. Most Wilderness First Aid books will tell you to keep your shoes on if the current is swift because the rocks on the streambed can be algae covered and slicker than greased owl shit. The first aid books don't actually say the "greased owl shit" part but you get the picture. No good if you're barefoot and barely good if you're not.

As Stilts had done many times before, he took off his boots to ford the stream. Instead of tying the shoelaces together and draping them around his neck as he normally did, he haphazardly rigged them to the outside of his backpack. About midway across one of his boots came loose, kerplunked in the water and deep-sixed like the Titanic. Stilts and his hiking partner spent the next hour searching for it, to no avail. His right boot was gone and it was 39 miles to Sonora Pass or 39 miles back to Tuolumne Meadows. He opted to walk back since he at least knew what the terrain would be like. He used a flip-flop padded with cushioning from his sleeping pad to make a shoe worthy of the 39-mile hike back to civilization. His boot is probably in the Pacific Ocean by now.

***

We woke up to our watch alarms at 6:00 A.M. I wiped the sleep from my eyes, unzipped my sleeping bag, threw on my shoes and walked over to the edge of Kerrick Creek. The water level had gone down at least a foot since last night. That was the good news. The bad news was that it was still a deep, ice-cold flow and we were going to have to cross it if we wanted make it to Canada before winter set in.

P.O.D. and Thumbs Up walked over to the edge of Kerrick Creek to take a look for themselves after I told them the water level had gone down. I could tell P.O.D. was still a bit squeamish at the thought of crossing it and frankly I was too.

We shouldered our packs and headed over for the crossing after gathering up two large and weighty sticks for P.O.D. We decided Thumbs Up and I would go first and then position ourselves on the opposite bank downstream of the crossing. P.O.D. would go last. The idea was to grab P.O.D. or hold a stick out for her to grab if she lost her footing and went in.

I was literally holding my breath as the next few minutes unfolded.

Both Thumbs Up and I were doling out as much positive reinforcement as possible. With each slow and methodically placed step, P.O.D. made her way to the middle of Kerrick Creek. From my field of vision a bit further downstream than Thumbs Up, the water appeared to be just about crotch-deep. I could tell by the wake forming on the upstream side of her leg that P.O.D. was definitely getting pushed by the force of the current. If she lost her footing or made one wrong move at this very second, she would be swept in.

"You got it P.O.D. Nice and easy," Thumbs Up said calmly from the far side of the bank.

P.O.D. gingerly planted her upstream hiking pole to the next spot and lifted her right leg to take the next step. She planted her foot firmly on the creek bottom and repeated with the downstream pole and left foot. The water level slowly moved down the length of her legs as she walked onto the far shore of Kerrick Creek. Thumbs Up and I breathed a collective sigh of relief. P.O.D. burst into tears. Tears of relief. And then she smiled, knowing that the obstacle she had been dreading for the last two and a half days was now in her rear-view mirror.

We wouldn't face any other stream crossings that came close to Kerrick Creek during the remaining 1,700 miles of our hike north to Canada. I think I speak for both of us by saying that we'd be just fine if we never crossed another snowmelt-swollen creek anywhere on the planet in early season for the rest of our lives. I can guarantee you that on our next thru-hike of the PCT (yes, there will definitely be another one) we will not leave Kennedy Meadows until the pre-calculated Kennedy Meadows Day. Even if George bites me again and the toilet is out of commission, I swear we will not leave.

9

A Hitchhiker's Guide to Maine

"Hurry up, get in."

I had a split second to make a decision on whether or not I was going to get into the rickety old 70's model Ford Bronco that had just come to a screeching halt in the gravel pullout I was standing in.

"How's it going?" I asked calmly from the passenger seat of this stranger's Bronco.

"Fine," the man said, sounding annoyed.

I kept quiet for a few minutes and started making mental preparations to pepper spray the guy's face or jump out of the moving truck if things went south. The only reason I was even in this guy's truck to begin with was because I needed a ride to the grocery store in Rangeley, Maine, to buy food for the next stretch of trail.

Hitchhiking on long-distance trails is a given and is one of my least favorite parts of walking long trails. Believe it or not, most hikers don't carry five months worth of food on their backs when heading out for a five-month hike. At a pound and a half of food a day, that would be 225 lbs of food.

To make things a bit more manageable, most long-distance hikers hitch to grocery stores once or twice a week. Once in a blue moon the trail will take you directly through a town, but more often than not, you reach an intersection where the trail crosses a paved road that leads a few miles distant to a town with a supermarket.

The typical scenario plays out like this: "Stormin' Norman" is on his Appalachian Trail thru-hike and has arrived at a spot where the AT crosses Highway such and such. The town of so and so is 10 miles east on this road, and according to Norman's guidebook, it has a big grocery store, hotels and a laundromat. Norman is almost out of food since his last grocery stop five days ago and he hasn't taken a shower for the better part of a month. Stormin' Norman sticks out his thumb and hitches a ride to the grocery store. He gets picked up by a local that knows about the AT and recognizes him as an AT thru-hiker. Norman gets dropped off right at the front door of the grocery store and the driver wishes him well and politely suggests he consider a bath while in town.

I've found that carrying a small piece of poster board that says "Friendly Hiker to Town" often helps in getting a ride. So does hitching with a woman. I've even had the same folks that dropped me off also offer to give me a ride back to the trail after I finished shopping. On the PCT in 2004 my hiking partner and I were offered a place to stay for the night and showers by an older couple that were giving us a ride from the dusty town of Onyx back to the PCT. I declined because "we have eight more miles to hike today" and am still kicking myself for passing up a free shower and bed. Sometimes the pull to lay down miles clouds rational thinking. I even met a guy who was so blown away that we were walking from Mexico to Canada along the Pacific Crest Trail that he insisted on treating three of us to lunch in a nearby town.

Luckily for me, the guy in the Ford Bronco was just in a hurry. He eventually told me that he had hiked the Appalachian Trail a decade prior although his story seemed to have a few holes in it. I didn't challenge him though; no need to piss him off as I was just happy to be getting a ride and relieved that he wasn't a psychopath.

I've been told by my mother since I was barely out of diapers that you never accept rides from strangers and you NEVER ever ever hitchhike because there are axe murderers out there that go around looking for unsuspecting hitchhikers. Many other folks have backed up her statements, saying hitchhiking is too dangerous these days. "There are too many whackos out there," my Dad, who is a veteran hitchhiker himself, once told me.

Back in the 70's when "things were safe," my Dad hitchhiked from Florida to California and back with his parents' blessing. He ended up 90 miles from his hometown of Gainesville, Florida, and couldn't get a ride home after months of being on the road. That was the only rough spot he encountered during an entire summer's worth of hitching around the country.

The thing about hitching is that you never know what type of person is going to pick you up. And therein lies the risk. It's got to be someone who has not bought into the normal line of thinking that hitchhikers are axe murderers . . . or perhaps they are an axe murderer themselves. Sometimes I lay awake in my tent and play through the scenario of the driver and the hitchhiker both being axe murderers. Who would win? Regardless, I almost never pick up hitchhikers unless I know I'm near a hiking trail and feel pretty sure that the person with their thumb out is a backpacker. I also check to make sure they are not carrying an axe.

I had gotten into the habit of carrying a small bottle of pepper spray in my shorts pocket during any hitch while on trail. I'd keep the safety off and a lot of times I'd ride with my hand in my pocket and my finger on the trigger. It's better to be safe than sorry and I had guessed that getting into cars with strangers significantly increased my odds of being sorry.

Most hikers, myself included, prefer riding in the backs of trucks. That way there is a bit of separation between the driver and myself. Never mind that if the driver has a wreck or runs off the road I would surely be done for or that riding in the back of trucks is illegal in most states (except most of the Confederacy for some odd reason).

***

Gorham is the last town that hikers cross in New Hampshire before entering Maine. Most hikers take a few days off in Gorham to recover from having just traversed the White Mountains . . . one of the toughest mountain ranges on the entire AT. I was feeling a bit battered by the time I got there - partly because of how tough the hiking had been over the last week in the Whites and partly because I had literally just run for my life down Mt. Madison to the road at Pinkham Notch to avoid being struck by lightning. A nasty thunderstorm had moved onto the mountaintops and I was just minutes ahead of the impending doom that it was unleashing. Trying to outrun lightning is mostly futile but I made it to Gorham unscathed.

After leaving Gorham, my stomach started to feel queasy. Really queasy. I lost my appetite, which is extremely odd for someone who spent the better part of most days on the trail dreaming of all the food he would eat at the next town stop. The other thing that happened is that my stomach was bloated, big and puffy. And then there was the heinous gas. The kind of gas that could clear a room in a matter of seconds. The kind of gas that had been banned in the Kyoto Protocol. Bad, bad, gas.

I hiked a lot by myself during this stretch of trail as I didn't want to subject any of my fellow hikers to these noxious emissions. The day before I got to Andover, Maine, I had to force down every bite of food as I was not the least bit hungry and had been feeling rather nauseous in addition to my other symptoms. I figured it was just a stomach bug of some kind. "It'll be gone soon," I told myself.

There is an eight-mile hitch to get into Andover from the trail and just before I got to the road, my stomach went into a full revolt. I pulled into the woods and proceeded to cast out the demons, which had wrought hell on me the past few days. I felt a bit woosy during the next hour but luckily was able to get a quick hitch to the Pine Ellis Bed and Breakfast.

The Pine Ellis was a great little home nestled into the woods on the edge of Andover. It was just what I needed given my current state of affairs. I splurged for my own private room. This would be the first time I had stayed in my own room by myself in over four months of hiking. If there was a time that I needed it, that time was now. My stomach was upside down and I did not feel well at all.

I took two and a half days off while I was there. Most of that time was spent lying around, drinking ginger ale, eating saltines . . . all the usual stuff to settle an unsettled stomach. I seesawed between feeling nauseous to occupying the Pine Ellis throne to feeling nauseous again. If I had been a woman, I probably would have purchased a pregnancy test to find out why I had morning sickness.

I hit the trail again after 2 ½ days of rest in Andover but still didn't feel quite right. I just chalked it up to having hiked 1,800 miles and being a bit worked by the whole experience. On our second day out, I stopped to take a break at Sabbath Day Pond Lean-to – one of the many three-sided shelters along the AT in Maine. There was a small white poster in the shelter that had the title "Giardia Symptoms." It read: Diarrhea, bloating, flatulence, nausea, stomach cramps, fatigue and weight loss. Well, that's interesting, I thought . . . I had every one of those symptoms.

Still trying to convince myself that it was just a stomach bug, I stopped in Rangeley, the next trail town, for only a brief instance to pick up more groceries. I immediately got back on the trail and that night I camped with a bunch of hikers at Piazza Rock Lean-to. My buddy "Grubby" had packed in some Guinness and other hikers had also packed in beer. I'm a big fan of beer in general, but on the trail in the middle of nowhere, I'm especially a big fan of beer. There is nothing like a couple of tall ones to make sitting around a campfire that much more splendid. Much to my chagrin, I could barely get down one beer. This is when I knew that something was desperately wrong.

We spent the next couple of days traversing the Saddleback Mountains. The Saddlebacks are one of the most scenic mountain ranges in the Pine Tree state and it was all I could do not to fall over in a heap on the side of the trail. I don't remember much about the Saddlebacks. I kept my head down and focused on my footing with a stomach so nauseous I had trouble doing much other than thinking about which bush I could puke in. Time to go see a doctor. I had officially thrown in the towel.

Our next town stop was the hamlet of Stratton. There's not much going in on Stratton . . . a post office, couple of restaurants, couple of motels . . . that's about it. And no doctor's office I soon found out. The closest doctor's office was in Rangeley. Ugh. I had just been in Rangeley and had avoided the doctor's office because I had been in denial. And now I would have to hitch a ride(s) back to Rangeley and then hitch another set of rides back to Stratton. What a royal pain in the ass . . . and I had no one to blame but myself.

I got a room at the famed White Wolf Inn (home of the "Wolf Burger" – a thru-hiker favorite) for the night. My plan was to get up early and thumb a ride south to Rangeley. It was roughly a 20-mile hitch to get to Rangeley so I figured it'd be no problem. I headed out of my motel room and walked five minutes down to the intersection of Hwy 27 and Hwy 16 and put my thumb out. It was a Friday and there was a bit of traffic but not as much as I had hoped for. This area of Maine is fairly remote and doesn't see a whole lot of people until winter when it does it's biggest business with folks coming to Sugarloaf for ski vacation.

I was getting a bit discouraged after almost thirty minutes of standing by the side of the road, smiling, with my thumb out. I was clean, after all, and didn't smell of hiker filth. A big blue Oldsmobile turned down the road and immediately pulled over for me. Yahtzee!

I walked over to the window, which the woman in the passenger's seat was rolling down.

"I'm heading to the doctor's office in Rangeley," I offered.

"We're heading to Rangeley. Hop in back with the girls," the guy in the driver's seat retorted.

I peered into the backseat to see two young girls . . . probably in kindergarten or first grade. They smiled at me and continued to play with their dolls. They had absolutely no concern about a complete stranger getting into the back seat with them and were more than happy to share.

"My doll's name is Sandy," the younger of the two told me.

"This is Betsy," said the older girl as she held her doll three inches from my nose for me to see.

"Those are nice dolls," I told both of them.

The lady in the front was smoking a long skinny cigarette and the man driving looked like he had had a rough night. Not wanting to pry, but wanting them to know I was grateful for the ride I said, "I really appreciate you all giving me a ride. I've been hiking the Appalachian Trail and have had an upset stomach for weeks. I figured I'd better see a doctor."

"Hiking the AT, huh. You doin' the whole thing?" the man asked.

"Hoping to," I replied, not knowing whether I was going to make it all the way to the end even though I was only a few weeks shy of Mount Katahdin.

And that was about it for the next ten minutes or so. The man went on driving, the lady went on smoking and the two girls went about playing with their dolls. Sometimes silences can be uncomfortable so I just looked out the window and kept quiet, hoping the ride wouldn't take too long.

After double-checking my wallet for cash, I glanced back out the windshield just in time to see a great blue heron flying in the direction of the car. Great blue heron's are sizeable birds, the largest of the herons in North America, as a matter of fact. They can grow up to 4 ½ feet from head to toe and boast wingspans of over six feet. Luckily they don't get more than eight pounds or so in weight because when that bird hit the windshield, it looked as if a pterodactyl had just landed on the car.

It bounced off the windshield and was slingshot to the side of the road. I involuntarily ducked and then quickly looked up at the man and woman. They didn't flinch. The guy just kept driving, gazing out the windshield as he had been doing before being struck by a large heron. The woman continued smoking and thumping her ashes out the cracked passenger-side window every once in a while. The girls continued to play with their dolls and nobody looked at me. They all acted as if nothing had happened.

Perhaps I was delirious from weeks of giardiasis. Perhaps a large heron did not hit the windshield and almost run us off the road. No one else seemed to have noticed. Was I losing my mind? Was I in some kind of stomach parasite-induced stupor? I thought about saying something . . . asking the driver if he was alright or the lady if she needed another cigarette . . . something, anything to make sure I wasn't seeing things! I kept mum though. The whole thing seemed a bit odd - like an episode of the *Twilight Zone*. If a small sparrow had flown into the car I could see it being no big deal, but this was a giant freaking blue bird.

We drove down the road in silence and only after five more minutes was a word spoken. The driver turned around to me quickly and said, "Sorry about that, there was nothing I could do." He turned back around and that was it. That's all that was said. The wife looked on with her cig in hand and the girls were chattering to their dolls. We had just collided with the largest of the North American herons, nearly had the windshield collapse in the car and almost ran off the road. Perhaps this is a common occurrence on the drive from Stratton to Rangeley. I checked the side of the road to see if it was littered with heron carcasses – none.

The man pulled the car over at the junction with Highway 4. He told me that he was headed in the opposite direction from that intersection. The junction was about four miles from the medical clinic and I really was hoping for a ride all the way, but was glad to get out of the car. I noticed a few feathers under the wipers as I waved goodbye to the Oldsmobile.

My suspicions were confirmed at the doctor's office. I had all the symptoms of a giardia infection and the doc prescribed some meds for me. I had been carrying a full course of the exact same meds in my pack for the last four months, which seemed a bit ironic. The doc made me feel slightly less like an imbecile when she told me that I likely needed a fresh batch since the meds I had been carrying had been outside for so long.

It took me another three hitches to get back to the White Wolf Inn. I spent the next few days eating pills and recuperating in my motel room. Within 36 hours, I felt about 80% better. My stomach had deflated to look less like a balloon and more like a football. The nausea was gone (thank God) and I actually had somewhat of an appetite again although there was no way I was going to try and eat the Wolf Burger.

In all reality though I needed some major time off, like the rest of the summer kind of time off. If I hadn't of had only 190 miles to go, I probably would have gone home early, but alas, I plugged away to Katahdin. And never again have I been in a car that had a head-on collision with a great blue heron.

10

On Luck's Side

The Glacier Peak Wilderness in northern Washington is one of the most rugged and formidable expanses of woodlands in the Pacific Northwest. It's an area that is 35 miles long and 20 miles wide and does not contain a single road. Crossing three entire counties and two national forests, Glacier Peak Wilderness is characterized by heavily forested slopes, steep valleys and the perpetual ice of remnant glaciers.

On October 23rd, 2003, Glacier Peak Wilderness experienced a colossal rain event that dropped 10 inches of rain in 10 hours. The pounding rain melted snow and ice, pushing enormous amounts of water, trees and debris into rivers and streams throughout the Wilderness Area. Extensive damage was wrought on lower elevation forests downstream from the high peaks. Roads, bridges, campgrounds and trails were overrun and destroyed. The Pacific Crest Trail didn't escape harm, either.

The PCT traverses the Glacier Peak Wilderness on the west side of the area's namesake, Glacier Peak. This west side of 10,500' Glacier Peak sustained significant damage during the 10-hour deluge and eight footbridges over a 30-mile section of the PCT were washed away. Little to no indication remains that these bridges ever existed. They were literally broken apart like toothpicks.

Bridges over the Upper White Chuck River and the Suiattle River were the biggest losses as both crossings are treacherous fords under the best of conditions. Even trails providing access to the PCT were not spared. Varying degrees of damage were delivered to the North Fork Skykomish Trail and the White Chuck Trail among others. Kennedy Hot Springs, a thru-hiker favorite along the route, was buried in a mudslide and rendered unusable.

Almost as quickly as the PCT was destroyed, talk of reconstructing it began. Oddly enough, one of the biggest obstacles with redeveloping the obliterated trail through this area of northern Washington was its Wilderness designation. The very designation that protects the area from all manner of intrusions such as logging and mining also makes it illegal to use any motorized equipment for trail repair. No chainsaws or weed eaters. No helicopters bringing in supplies or ATV access for trail crews. Everything would have to be done by hand and all supplies would be carried in on foot. The reconstruction effort would be run by trail crews camping out along the PCT for weeks at a time. The other issue of bringing this 30-mile trail segment back to life would be one of money.

Over the last decade, the US Forest Service has seen half of its annual budget go towards fighting and suppressing wildfires. In the last few years, the costs of fighting fires exceeded the money that was budgeted for this purpose. This led to money getting pulled from forest recreation and forest health programs to fund fighting fires. Given this reality, there was not much in the way of extra cash available to repair the PCT in the aftermath of the flooding in Glacier Peak Wilderness.

A year after the flood on my first thru-hike of the PCT in 2004, we were all told by the Forest Service that the "original PCT" through this area no longer existed. Hikers were encouraged to take an alternate hiking route or the official equestrian route. The alternate hiking route contained more up and down than the original trail route and it utilized trails that were unmaintained and overgrown and even more remote than the PCT. On more than one occasion, hikers who had taken the alternate route had reported fording two rivers that "made me fear for my life." Another thru-hiker later told me that she had lost the trail a half dozen times due to the lack of maintenance. "It's like *Jurassic Park* back there," were her exact words. By the time we arrived at the brink of Glacier Peak Wilderness in 2004, the forecast predicted snow for the following week so we opted to forgo the alternate hiking route for the more direct and less remote equestrian route.

The Pacific Crest Trail Association (PCTA), the non-profit overseeing the PCT's routing and volunteer maintenance projects, designated separate equestrian routes in various places throughout the length of the trail. Typically this occurred in areas where riding horses posed a significant danger both to the horse and to the rider - sections of narrow trail with steep cliffs and vertical drop-offs that would make you shit your knickers if you were on a horse next to a 1,000' drop off while trying to turn Mr. Ed around.

The equestrian route took us along paved and dirt road shoulders as we made our way around the east side of Glacier Peak Wilderness. Eventually we ducked off a dirt road onto a side trail, which rejoined with the PCT north of the huge section that had been destroyed in the flood. If it wasn't for the fact that about eight of us hoofed it through this detour together, it would have been one of the most boring stretches on my entire PCT hike. I would imagine that even horses would find the road walk a bit dull.

A fire in 2007 closed the hiker alternate route and left PCT'ers with a choice of doing the road walk/equestrian route or heading back onto the original PCT. A few 2006 hikers had hiked the original PCT and made it out alive. Word got around and a much higher percentage hiked the original trail the following year in 2007, including our friends "The Noodleheads" who told us first hand it was doable.

By early summer of 2008, we had read that new bridges had been installed in the majority of spots where bridges had previously been washed out. We were also warned that the going would be slow, particularly in a seven-mile stretch that contained 400+ old-growth blow downs. The Noodleheads said it was akin to going up and over a jungle gym a couple hundred times.

With that knowledge, and an extra map, we headed out of Stevens Pass on the original PCT into the Glacier Peak Wilderness. It started raining within a few hours of hitting the trail and in the next 24 hours, four hikers would turn back due to showing signs of early stage hypothermia.

P.O.D. and I kept a good pace all day and made it into Pear Lake before dark to cook dinner. We made quick work of a dinner of rice and beans while shooting the breeze with our friend "Wasa." After a big dinner, he had decided he would camp there for the night. We decided to press on a couple of miles while the weather was still clear. It didn't take long though before the rain started again and darkness fell. By the time we set up our tarp for the night, it was pouring.

Wasa caught up to us fairly quickly the next morning and told us that things got a bit interesting after we left Pear Lake. Two solo hikers and a couple had shown up to camp along the lake's shore after we left. There was a bit of an exposed camping area where we had cooked dinner containing flat ground that was just slightly softer than cement.

The hard ground wouldn't soak up any of the rain. Dozens of puddles formed and during the downpour, the couple's tent flooded. One of the solo hikers had a "waterproof" bivy. It leaked on him all night. And the other guy who camped there was a PCT thru-hiker named "Skinny." Skinny really, and I mean really, liked to brag to everyone about how amazingly light his backpack was. Many hikers spend thousands of dollars to buy the lightest gear possible. Skinny just didn't carry the gear. He had no tent - only a plastic painters tarp that he professed could be rigged between two trees to form an a-frame. He had no real rain gear; instead, he cut holes in a trash bag that allowed him to wear it as kind of a rain toga. And he had a 40-degree sleeping bag - barely warm enough is putting it nicely considering the frost we had all been waking up to the past week in northern Washington.

That night at Pear Lake, Skinny set up his "camp" on the hard ground next to everyone else. In his hurry to string up his painter's tarp, he failed to notice the spot he had chosen was in a slight depression. Within a few hours, Skinny's entire camp-site was submerged in one big dirty puddle. He could do nothing more than wrap himself up in his painters plastic like a burrito while watching the water funnel into his down sleeping bag.

The other solo hiker and the couple turned back the next morning. They decided that it would be too dangerous to continue with shelters that leaked and gear that was soaked given that the forecast for the next five days was calling for rain. Lots of rain. Skinny, however, decided to hike on. It baffles me to this day why he kept going. Sometimes the pull of the trail and continuing the journey towards Canada can cloud any remnant of rational thought amongst PCT hikers.

That morning Skinny packed up his things at first light and hiked out of his flooded campsite. He passed by our tarp without our noticing him. We had decided to sleep in a bit, not interested in hiking out into the cold wet morning while we slumbered cozy and dry in our toasty sleeping bags.

When we finally caught up with Skinny later in the morning, I knew he had spent a very long night without much sleep. He was standing off the side of the trail under a tree wearing his trash bag toga. His cotton floppy hat was totally soaked and he had bags under his eyes.

"How's it going Skinny?" I offered up trying not to sound too glum.

"Pretty rough. I didn't sleep at all last night and my sleeping bag is soaked. I'm hoping to find a cave to dry my gear in," he told us.

I thought to myself that this plan sounded fairly horrendous. He was entirely soaked, didn't have a real shelter to camp under, his down sleeping bag was drenched and he figured he would magically find a cave in which to dry out his gear. Perhaps the cave would have a magical fire already blazing inside it and a warm set of dry clothes neatly folded in the corner for just such an occasion. And the Swedish women's volleyball team would surely be there using the cave for a vision quest.

I immediately had visions of Skinny becoming hypothermic at some point during the day. An old Wilderness First Aid guide I have states that one of the easiest ways to bring the body temperature of a hypothermic person back up to normal is to get into a sleeping bag naked with them. I had absolutely no interest in getting into a sleeping bag naked with Skinny. Zero. Amongst other things, Skinny was not very skinny. I'm six foot two and I doubt there is a sleeping bag big enough to contain both Skinny and I. Perhaps I was overreacting, though, and Skinny would find his magical cave.

After an hour or so we stopped to take a snack break and Skinny staggered up behind us. He didn't look good. He pulled out his sleeping bag to show us what had happened to it. It looked like a loaf of wet bread. The thing about down feathers is that when they get wet, they are absolutely useless as an insulator. They flatten and it takes hours upon hours to dry them out. I've spent half-days waiting for a commercial dryer to get all the dampness out of down sleeping bags that I washed.

Skinny mentioned finding a cave again. Then he said if he got too cold, he would hike through the night. With that, he took off. I looked at my watch and it was getting close to noon. I told P.O.D. that Skinny was going to be in a lot of trouble tonight if he kept hiking on. And then I thought again of having to crawl in a sleeping bag naked with him in order to save his life.

Within thirty minutes we happened upon Skinny again. He was sitting on the side of the trail under a tree soaking wet as the rain poured down on him. His sleeping bag was lying on the ground beside him in the dirt. It resembled a wet sponge that had just been used to wipe mud off a pair of filthy boots. P.O.D. was a few steps ahead of me and we almost walked by him with nothing more than a wave. Something told me to stop and I froze in my tracks. I needed to talk some sense into Skinny. I needed to get him to turn around and go back to the road and hitch back down the highway to the town of Skykomish. And I needed him not to end up in an emergency situation that involved having no clothes on in a sleeping bag with me!

"Skinny" I said gravely, "You are in a dangerous situation. You are soaking wet, your down sleeping bag is soaking wet and you have no tent or tarp. It's supposed to rain all week and we are 75 miles from Stehekin. If you keep going, you are going to become hypothermic tonight."

I was a bit surprised at how blunt it sounded and could tell that I had caught his attention.

"If I were in your shoes, I would turn around and hike back to Stevens Pass right now and hitch back down to Skykomish. You can dry out all your gear there and wait for this weather to pass."

At that moment Wasa walked up and, realizing the gravity of the situation, he too piped in and strongly encouraged Skinny to go back to Skykomish.

Sometimes it just takes someone saying something out loud for it to become acceptable.

"Yeah. I was thinking maybe I should go back. I can dry out all my gear and get a better shelter," Skinny said as if a light bulb had just been flicked on in his brain.

"You know the Dinsmores in Skykomish will let you stay at their house as long as you need. You'll get a hitch pretty quickly," I offered, to reinforce his decision to turn back. The Dinsmores were local trail angels in Skykomish that offered hikers a place to stay and shower.

Skinny gathered up his drenched sleeping bag and some other gear that he had strewn about on the wet ground beside him, shouldered his pack and headed back towards the road. I breathed more than one sigh of relief as we headed north from Skinny's break spot knowing I'd be solo in my own sleeping bag tonight.

For the next four days it rained off and on as we made our way to Stehekin . . . the last town stop on the PCT. We encountered various degrees of new trail construction and found six of the eight footbridges had been replaced. The other two streams not containing footbridges had huge fallen trees over them that served as de facto bridges. We were able to keep our feet dry and cross on the trees. And the stretch of trail that supposedly had 400+ downed old-growth trees only had about half that. I know because I counted. It was still slow going though. There's a lot of work left to do in Glacier Peak Wilderness before the trail is back to its original state. And I doubt that Kennedy Hot Springs will ever be unearthed as it's under about ten feet of dry mud at the moment.

***

Getting to the town of Stehekin requires a bus ride from the High Bridge Ranger Station down Stehekin River Road. The bus makes that trip four times a day and we decided to camp just shy of the ranger station in order to get the first bus into town the following morning.

We hiked down to the bus pickup spot early that next morning just as the sun was rising. I could see that the bus schedule was posted on the kiosk in front of the Ranger Station. I went over to double check the times and saw the following notice posted beside the schedule:

ATTENTION:

PCT THRU-HIKER "LUCKY"

"Lumber" and "Milkman" are concerned about you and are waiting for you at the Overflow Campground at the Stehekin Landing.

Posted August 29th 2008

My heart sank into my stomach. This was bad. This was really really bad. We knew Lucky. And we knew that Lucky and Lumber and Milkman and a few others were hiking together a few days in front of us when we left Stevens Pass. We had hiked with Lucky infrequently in the southern California section of the PCT and he was one of those hikers who carried only the *PCT Data Book* to navigate. No guidebook, no maps and no info other than the condensed spreadsheet of mileages and data points the *PCT Data Book* provided. We could only assume that Lucky had hiked into the Glacier Peak Wilderness with the same lack of maps and guidebooks.

The other thing is that PCT hikers don't get lost. They just don't. Sure we get "misplaced" from time to time and get ourselves back to the PCT as soon as we realize we took a wrong turn or happened down the wrong trail. But being lost for days in an expansive Wilderness Area when we're supposed to be laying down 20-30 miles per day in order to get to Canada . . . it just doesn't happen.

I specifically remember one conversation we had with Lucky a few months back. He told us that hanging around other hikers and listening to what they said was the easiest way to glean important info. This was how he found out where to hitch into the next town, where the good water sources were and just about every other vital piece of info one would need to hike the trail. If Lucky were lost out there without a map or guidebook, or any other hikers around, he'd be flying blind.

I walked back over to P.O.D. and we both went back and looked at the sign. The eight o'clock bus came rumbling up the road and we gathered our things to get aboard. Lumber and Milkman were the first people off the bus.

"Did you see Lucky?" Milkman asked us with tears in his eyes.

"No we didn't. What's going on?" I asked realizing very quickly that the situation was serious.

Both Milkman and Lumber looked as though they had just seen a ghost, spooked and in disbelief. They both spent the next few minutes relaying the entire sequence of events of the last week.

Apparently they had all hiked out of Stevens Pass together a few days before we did. The four of them that composed their group had camped together the first two nights. They had all been camping together since northern Oregon and had plans to finish out the last couple weeks on the trail as a group. On the third morning Lucky got up a bit earlier than everyone else and decided to hike out first. The rest of the crew left 15 minutes later and hadn't seen him since.

At first they assumed he had gotten antsy and took off to get to Stehekin early. However, none of the hikers they passed who were heading the opposite direction had seen him. By the time they got to Stehekin, they were more than worried. They checked the post office to see if Lucky had picked up the mail there waiting on him. He had not. He was not in Stehekin and they could only presume he was still in Glacier Peak Wilderness and lost.

Milkman and Lumber had their packs with them. After waiting around for Lucky for three days, they decided to hike out and finish the trip. They told us that they had been in touch with the park ranger at Stehekin and asked us to escalate the search and rescue.

The bus was getting ready to pull away so we had to cut the conversation short. We boarded the bus and sat down a bit thunderstruck as Milkman and Lumber hiked out, headed to Canada without Lucky. "What should we do?" I asked P.O.D.

The bus dropped us off at "the Landing," the spit of land where people hop on and off the ferry that transports tourists and year-round residents to Stehekin. Stehekin is one of the few towns in the lower 48 that in not accessible by road, only by boat or on foot. The boat comes across Lake Chelan from the town of Chelan three times a day. It's a long boat ride of about two hours each way. Lots of folks were heading into Stehekin as it was the start of the Labor Day weekend.

We immediately headed over to the National Park Service office to talk with Diane Hummel, the Law Enforcement Park Ranger that Milkman and Lumber had spoken to. I was in a bit of a fog as we walked up the stairs to the Park Service building. The last thought to cross my mind before we opened the entrance door was, "What would I want someone to do for me right now if I had been missing for four days?"

"We wanted to talk to you about the missing PCT hiker Lucky," I stated calmly to Ranger Hummel. "We know Lucky and if he is missing, it's probably not good."

I explained to her that he likely did not have any maps or guidebooks. She grew a bit concerned at this possibility. The weather had been really nasty back there all week. Although Lucky likely had rain gear and a good shelter, without a map and a way to navigate back to the trail, it could simply be a matter of time before he found himself in dire straits.

Diane told us that it wasn't uncommon for hikers to go missing and then show up a few days late. She said the Park Service saw this scenario play out all the time and I knew she was right. The only problem was that Lucky was a PCT thru-hiker. Thru-hikers don't just take off from their hiking partners and go missing for days on end. It just doesn't happen that way with us. I tried to convey that as plainly as possible, but I could tell that it didn't completely make sense to her.

She told us that they would wait to see if he showed up today. If he didn't, they would send a ranger up to the bus pickup spot at High Bridge Ranger Station that evening to see if Lucky had appeared after the last bus left. She also allowed us to see a copy of Lucky's home phone number, which Milkman had given to her. Additionally, she conferenced in Glen Bartram on her phone while we were in her office. Glen would be heading up the search and rescue (SAR) effort, which was just getting started.

The call was a bit garbled due to Stehekin being on an anti-quated satellite phone relay system. There was a 1-2 second delay between when you spoke and when the person on the other end of the staticky line heard you. There was no cell phone service at all so even though I was carrying a cell phone, I couldn't use it in Stehekin. P.O.D. did her best to explain everything we knew about Lucky to Glen in spite of the phone system. Glen was also concerned to hear that Lucky didn't have maps. In hindsight, I believe this single piece of info is what troubled the SAR folks the most.

For those of you who know the story of Chris McCandless in Jon Krakauer's *Into the Wild*, you will remember that Chris likely died of starvation in an abandoned bus in central Alaska. He had attempted to leave the bus earlier that summer on his way back out to civilization, but had been turned back by high water in the river he had crossed months before en route to the bus. Without a topographic map and presumably not knowing any other routes out of his location, he hiked back to the bus, stayed put and died. Almost no one knew where he was and no one was looking for him.

Granted, the PCT in Washington is not Alaska. Here we definitely had the advantage of lots of folks knowing about Lucky's situation, and search and rescue teams ready to go to the area where Lucky was last seen. Those SAR teams just needed the word and they'd be sent out.

We told Diane that we'd check back with her towards the end of the day and sooner if we heard any new info on Lucky's whereabouts. We headed back down to the Landing and walked over to the post office to pick up our maildrops.

The thought came back in my head as we picked up our maildrops from the post office, "What would I want someone doing for me right now if I had been missing for four days?" I honestly felt the weight of Lucky's situation had been placed square on our shoulders because of Milkman and Lumber's plea to us to escalate the search and rescue.

Calling someone's wife or husband to tell them that their spouse was missing and that the situation was bad is not a call anyone would ever want to make. P.O.D. and I both knew that a family member who had information that his or her spouse was missing would be the catalyst to get things done. In essence, we knew Lucky was likely in a bad situation and that we could only do so much to escalate the SAR effort ourselves. Lucky's wife could do a lot more. P.O.D. called Lucky's wife. To this day, I am still in awe of the strength she showed to make that call.

To our disbelief, Lucky's wife already knew what was going on even though she was 2,000 miles away in Michigan. She had just gotten off the phone with a sheriff from one of the local counties. So P.O.D. did not end up breaking the news to her, which was a relief. She told Lucky's wife everything we knew. Midway through the call they were both sobbing.

As it happens, P.O.D.'s parents live 15 minutes from Lucky's wife in Michigan. P.O.D. called her mom and dad and gave them Lucky's wife's home phone number. She explained the situation to her parents and asked them to call his wife to comfort her. We both thought it might help having P.O.D.'s parents call her since they knew us and knew about the situation that her husband was in.

I called the Dinsmores back in Skykomish to see if Lucky had shown up there. She told me he hadn't. I explained the entire situation to her, which took a long time given the phone delay and inadequate reception I was getting on Stehekin's one and only pay phone. I could tell she was really worried about Lucky's prospects. She told me that she and her husband Jerry would get on the phone with law enforcement there in Skykomish and get something going.

I hung up the phone and walked down to the road to clear my head a bit. It had been a complete whirlwind since I had boarded the bus to Stehekin at High Bridge Ranger Station. I felt quite helpless standing there on the road knowing that Lucky was out there and had been missing for over half a week. What was happening to him?

"What would I want someone doing for me right now?" raced across my brain once again. We had talked to Diane,

Glen, the Dinsmores, Lucky's wife and P.O.D.'s parents. The word was getting out but what was going to get Lucky found was a full-scale search and rescue effort. If I could do anything to help Lucky right now, it would be to make sure that the SAR effort got started as soon as possible. The SAR folks would be the ones that would find Lucky, not any of us.

There is an internet bulletin board that PCT hikers use heavily. It's called the "Pct-L" which simply means PCT List-serv. Lots of hikers post questions on Pct-L during the planning phases of their hikes in order to get info from other hikers who have already done the trail. The Pct-L gets a lot of traffic; anywhere from 20-30 posts a day when it's really humming. I could call one person at a time on the substandard satellite pay phone or I could post the entire situation on Pct-L and reach a much larger group of hikers that would be just as concerned about Lucky as I was.

I hesitated briefly in doing so because I've seen people get criticized and bashed on this listserv for saying something or doing something deemed inappropriate. I also knew that there was a good chance I would get criticized for posting Lucky's situation on Pct-L and asking folks to call the local sherrifs' offices to add a sense of urgency to the search and rescue effort. In the end, I decided that if I had been missing for four days, I would want someone to do the same for me. I logged onto the computer above the post office and typed the following email:

Subject: PCT Thru-Hiker Missing in Glacier Peak Wilderness-NEED HELP NOW

PCT-L,

PCT thru-hiker 'Lucky' has gone missing in the Glacier Peaks Wilderness Area. This is no joke and we need your help right now. I repeat, this is no joke. This is Disco and I'm in Stehekin right now with P.O.D., Wasa and a few other thru-hikers. P.O.D. and I just got to Stehekin this morning to find out that Lucky has not been seen since Tuesday morning. Today is Saturday so it has been 4 full days now. His wife has been contacted and we think (and hope) that Search and Rescue efforts are underway or at least getting started right now but there does not seem to be a sense of urgency about the situation with the authorities we have talked to thus far. The Dinsmores are also aware of the situation and have contacted a sheriff (not sure which county).

Here is what I know as of right now (2:00 P.M. Saturday). Lucky had been hiking with two other thru-hikers coming out of Stevens Pass heading north on the PCT. All three of them camped just south of White Pass on Monday night. Keep in mind that the White Pass I'm referring to here is the one on trail in Glacier Peak Wilderness just south of Red Pass (not the one with the ski resort in southern Washington that hikers pick up packages at). So they were all camped together Monday night and then Tuesday morning they got up and Lucky hiked out about 15 minutes before the other 2 did. The other two hikers have not seen him since. P.O.D. and I were about 1.5 days behind them and we did not see Lucky nor has anyone else at this point. Lucky and the two hikers he was with took the original PCT thru this section as did we. The weather the last couple of days has been rainy, foggy, windy and cold. The two hikers that Lucky was with think he may have gotten to White Pass and then taken a wrong trail down to the North Fork Sauk River. The PCT on White Pass is above treeline and has at least two junctions that aren't marked or signed very well and if you are up there in the fog and the rain, it would be real easy to end up taking the wrong trail. The North Fork Sauk River Trail heads down off White Pass to the west and eventually hits a forest service road and then the town of Bedal, which is on Mountain Loop Highway. Bedal is just south of the town of Darrington. My other thought is that he may have possibly headed east down the FT 1507 trail that goes down the White River and on over to Boulder Pass and Little Giant Pass?

The bottom line is that he was due in Stehekin on Thursday and hasn't been seen since Tuesday morning. His hiking partners told us that he had a lot of food with him but that he was only carrying the PCT Data Book and possibly the PCT guidebook. But we all know that the maps in the guidebook are for the narrow PCT corridor and wouldn't help that much if he got way off trail. White Pass serves as the county border between Chelan and Snohomish counties. Chelan county is to the east and Snohomish county is to the west. Wenatchee National Forest & Glacier Peak Wilderness are to the east and Mount Baker-Snoqualmie National Forest & Henry M. Jackson Wilderness are to the west.

Can someone with phone access call both the sheriff for Chelan county and Snohomish county to make sure they are escalating the search and rescue effort for Lucky. Can someone also call both national forest ranger offices that I just listed above and inquire about search and rescue for Lucky.

I hiked with Lucky and know he is a competent hiker and has a lot of food but he might need our help right now. I'm flying blind here in Stehekin. We met with the park service law enforcement ranger this morning (I think her name is Diane). She has made some phone calls but the feeling I get is that this is serious business considering that Lucky hasn't been seen in 4 days and there needs to be a full scale search and rescue effort going on right now and from what I can tell that has yet to happen. If you have any information on Lucky's whereabouts, please contact the Dinsmores and or the North Cascades National Park office in Stehekin.

Thank you, Disco

I hit send and that was it. I just made the entire situation known to the Pct-L and had asked anyone concerned to escalate the situation for better or worse. My only hope is that it would help Lucky get found more quickly.

There wasn't much to do at this point but sit around and wait. My nerves were on edge as we sat in the little community room above the post office watching TV. It was getting dark and there was still no sign of Lucky. What was his wife thinking right now? What preparations were the SAR folks making? Was Lucky alive?

I continued to monitor the Pct-L for any information on Lucky and within three hours, a former PCT thru-hiker posted the following message on pct-l:

I have talked to the Darrington Ranger District two times now. The Search and rescue is being overwhelmed by calls. There is a full-fledged Search and Rescue under way ("We are all over this"), Helicopters are standing by and waiting for enough visibility. A description has been sent to a person on Miners Ridge to sit lookout on the PCT on that side. A second person is on the original PCT at Milk creek - so that both PCT branches are being watched for Lucky. The N. Fork Sauk road is closed at Bedal, this closure is 7.3 miles from the N. Fork Sauk creek trailhead that Lucky would have descended if he went that way. There are SAR crews that have already started from multiple trailheads and multiple directions. They are doing everything they can and fully realize this is not a false alarm. My prayers are with you all, and of course, Lucky.

Tears welled up in my eyes and I got up from the computer, walked into the men's bathroom (which was thankfully vacant) and I cried. I was so relieved that the SAR effort had started in earnest for Lucky. I was relieved for his wife. I was relieved for us. And I was relieved for him. We had no idea what he was going through, but we knew that if he was out there, he would be found one way or another.

I splashed some water on my face, wiped my eyes with a paper towel and breathed a deep sigh of relief. It was out of our hands completely now and in the hands of people that could and would actually find Lucky. Later I would find out that the story had been broadcast on the Seattle nightly news. If there were any doubts that Lucky's situation was not gaining attention, those doubts were gone.

As I walked back to my tent from the community room, I knew Lucky was dead. Tomorrow would be the fifth day that he had been missing. If he had taken that faint trail from White Pass to the northeast and up to the glaciers, my gut feeling was that SAR volunteers would be doing a body recovery at best. I felt sick to my stomach that night as I tried to fall asleep in my tent.

The next morning dawned calm and sunny. It would be a good weather day for the SAR teams. As we were boarding the eight o'clock bus to the Stehekin Bakery for breakfast, I knew search and rescue efforts were underway. I also knew that there were a lot of people around the country that had high hopes that Lucky would be found today.

We arrived at the bakery to find our friend Wasa. He had gotten up early and walked there. After ordering a handful of pastries, we talked with Wasa about everything that had happened since arriving in Stehekin. He held out as little hope as I did that Lucky would be found alive. We went over the entire week's happenings in Glacier Peak Wilderness: the couple whose tent flooded, the guy whose bivy sack leaked, Skinny's near hypothermia and now Lucky. This had been a dreadful week for hikers in Washington. It made me question being out there with ultralight gear. Were we pushing the envelope a bit too much? We had a tarp and not a lot in the way of extra clothing. If we fell in a stream or river and our gear got soaked, would we be any better off than Skinny or the other folks that got flooded out?

I heard the rumble of the nine o'clock bus pulling into the bakery from High Bridge Ranger Station and was curious to see if there were any thru-hikers on it. Perhaps someone who had seen Lucky? I peered out the window to see who was getting off the bus. P.O.D. had walked over towards the door to get a closer look when I heard her exclaim, "Damn! It's Lucky."

I turned to the door to see a bedraggled Lucky walk right in wearing his pack. My jaw nearly hit the floor. It was literally like looking at a ghost. Tears welled up in my eyes again as we all ran over to Lucky to find out what had happened. He looked rough - really rough, like a person who hadn't slept in weeks.

It was Sunday, August 31st. Lucky left Stevens Pass a week ago on Sunday, August 24th and had planned to be in Stehekin on Thursday. He was 72 hours late. But he was alive. We were beyond relief.

We gave Lucky enough time to buy a box load of pastries. He was famished and for good reason as we would find out. He came back to our table and between wolfing down a couple of days worth of pastries in one sitting, he told us of the harrowing week he just spent in the Glacier Peak Wilderness.

He had hiked out of camp Tuesday morning about fifteen minutes before everyone else. It was foggy when he arrived on White Pass. Half a mile later he came to a trail junction and took the wrong trail. He descended the unsigned North Fork Sauk River Trail leading to the North Fork Sauk River. After 45 minutes of descending and not remembering a big descent in the *PCT Data Book*, he stopped and skimmed to the page with White Pass on it. He saw that the PCT did not descend from White Pass; it ascends some 550 feet to Red Pass. Knowing that he had taken the wrong trail, he turned around and hiked back to the PCT but had already lost an hour and a half by the time he got back to the trail junction. Knowing that his buddies were up ahead, he picked up the pace but it just wasn't enough to catch them by the end of the day. He set up camp and decided he would get an early start the next morning to try to catch them.

Lucky woke up to more drizzle and fog the following morning. It was Wednesday and he felt he would be able to catch his hiking partners and still get into Stehekin by Thursday evening. He skipped his normal breaks and hiked hard all day, reaching Milk Creek by mid-afternoon. Coming into Milk Creek, the navigating got tough. The trail was overgrown and washed out in numerous places due to the 2003 flood. When we hiked through this section, we found it easier to bushwhack down to the trail if we could see it below us rather than climbing up and over downed trees or trying to scamper across a steeply sloping mudslide. When Lucky came through this section it was raining and foggy. Just before reaching Milk Creek, the trail literally dead-ended high above its swift flowing waters because the 2003 flood washed away a large portion of its banks. A scramble down to the creek bed was needed to reach the spot where the PCT footbridge crossed Milk Creek. What was left of the bridge was still there but had been literally broken in half as if a huge boulder had been hurled from the sky right onto the middle of it. We were able to use it to cross Milk Creek and had it not been for the still intact wooden handrails on each side of the foot-wide bridge, we would have been forced to ford Milk Creek. This would have been a desperate move at best given how fast it was flowing.

Lucky bushwacked downhill to the creek and ended up about 50' downstream from the bridge. Visibility was about 10-20' in the dense foggy rain and when he reached the cold silty water, he couldn't see the bridge upstream. He wasn't even sure he was at Milk Creek.

He rightfully assumed that the PCT would cross Milk Creek on a bridge; however, he concluded that he just needed to walk downstream to find that bridge. So he walked downstream for the next few hours searching for a bridge that had only been 50' upstream from where he first hit water's edge. There was a remnant trail that kept appearing and disappearing as he made his way downstream and he assumed this was the PCT. It was actually the Milk Creek Trail, which ultimately led down to a distant larger river and away from the PCT.

Darkness closed in on him and he decided the best thing to do was to set up camp for the night. It was raining and he wasn't sure where he was and decided night hiking in the rain along the creek would be futile. The only problem was that the stream banks on either side of Milk Creek were steeply slanted and a bit overgrown. He would have to set up his tent in Milk

Creek's drainage and hope the water did not rise too much overnight. If it did rise, he would have to abandon his camp and hike in the dark in pouring rain in order to find level ground and a suitable camp.

Around 2:00 A.M., the creek had risen enough to come in under his tent just slightly. Lucky's down sleeping bag started to take on water. He piled some extra stuffsacks and his waterproof pack cover around the edges of his sleeping bag to minimize the bag's contact with water. He was able to eek out about ten minutes of sleep after being confronted with the realization that rising waters could spell disaster. At 5:00 A.M. he decided to pack up and hike out. He still did not know where the bridge was and continued to believe it was downhill.

He spent the bulk of the morning hiking down washed out Milk Creek drainage. He forded and reforded silty Milk Creek numerous times and in the process ended up soaked from the waist down. The on and off rain and windy conditions made hypothermia a real possibility and Lucky kept moving in order to stay warm. By late morning, he took a break on a rock and studied his *PCT Data Book* once again. It just didn't seem right that he was continuing to descend with not much of a trail to be found and no footbridge anywhere in sight. He still wasn't sure he was even on Milk Creek and had no map to verify it. The data book showed a 2,000+ foot climb on the PCT coming out of the creek which didn't add up given that he had been descending for so long. Conceding that he was at Milk Creek heading downhill would mean that not only had he taken the wrong way by going down the creek's drainage, but also that he would have to go all the way back up, find the PCT and then do a 2,000+ foot climb. After mulling this over he came to the only logical conclusion that was possible - that in fact he was descending Milk Creek. With that, he turned around and began the long slow trudge, fording and refording the swift waters, as he made his way back to the point where he had initially come onto Milk Creek's banks.

The sky had cleared a bit but he did not recognize much of anything as his descent down Milk Creek had been spent mostly in a dense fog. By the end of the day he was worn out and a bit depressed that he had not found the PCT. What he didn't know was that he had actually ascended too high, crossing the PCT about 10 minutes before stopping for the night. He set up camp in a flat spot beside Milk Creek but high enough above it so he would not have to be concerned about another nighttime flood. Once again he made a smart choice in not night hiking even though he was growing a bit concerned about his circumstances. Feeling more than glum, he crawled into his damp sleeping bag and slept the bulk of the night.

Within five minutes of breaking camp the following morning, Lucky ran into a trail crew that was set up on the other side of Milk Creek a bit further up. Relieved and elated to see people, he quickly hiked over and asked them where the trail was. He couldn't believe it when they told him it was about 15 minutes back down the drainage. This crew had set up in one of the only large flat spots big enough to hold them and close enough to the PCT's crossing of Milk Creek to keep them from having to hike a long distance to reach the trail. They were there to repair the bridge and the trail. Somehow Lucky had missed the bridge again on his way back up. He asked the crew if they could radio a forest ranger to let them know that he likely had friends who were concerned about him and looking for him. The trail crew told him that they could not. They said they could only radio in for emergencies.

Lucky hurried back down the wash and found the bridge and the trail this time. Relieved and ecstatic, he took off but quickly realized there was no way he'd catch Milkman and Lumber before they got to Stehekin. He had lost a day and a half walking up and down Milk Creek drainage. It was now Friday and he had almost 40 miles to get to High Bridge Ranger Station and Stehekin. He had planned on getting to Stehekin on Thursday and his food was running low. Luckily he had packed extra but he'd likely be completely out by the time he got to High Bridge.

He ran into another trail crew around the Suiattle River, or at least the evidence that a trail crew was in the area. He found a large canvas tent with bunks and a kitchen tent with a low fire going. His bag was damp and he was hungry from rationing food and the promise of standing by a warm fire was exactly what he needed to dry his gear and lift his spirits. He pulled out his down sleeping bag and dried it by the fire as he cooked up one of his dinners. The trail crew came back just before dusk and Lucky tried to explain who he was and what he was doing, which was a bit tough to the all Spanish-speaking trail crew. They apparently concluded he was in rough shape and offered him a place to bunk for the night. They fed him two huge plates for dinner and a big breakfast the following morning. Lucky had hit the jackpot.

Just before he left their camp that next morning, he attempted to ask them to radio a forest ranger about his situation. Once again he tried to convey that he likely had friends who were worried about him and looking for him but it got lost in translation. He hiked out with a full stomach and renewed energy and covered the almost 27 miles to High Bridge Ranger Station by the end of the day. Unfortunately for Lucky, the last bus back to Stehekin left at five o'clock and he didn't arrive until six. It was Saturday night and he thought maybe someone would show up and he could possibly bum a ride back to town. What he didn't know is that a search and rescue effort was being assembled on his behalf and that the park service was going to send someone up to check High Bridge one last time before the end of the night. That never happened and no tourists or locals decided to make the trip to the ranger station in the dark. Essentially, no one knew that Lucky was safe and had made it to High Bridge. He would have to overnight there and wait for the first bus to town the following morning.

Lucky was truly lucky that he made it out alive. He made a number of good decisions after being lost twice and avoided some bad ones. He had carried extra food with him and didn't hike at night in the rain. He did, however, hike out of Stevens Pass with no maps and no guidebooks, which I later confirmed with him. Thru-hikers can become complacent after having followed a well-marked and well-maintained national scenic trail for months on end. The problem with this type of complacency is that the post-flood PCT through Glacier Peak Wilderness was neither well-marked nor well-maintained. It had been virtually obliterated only five years prior and had a ways to go before it was back to its original condition.

The search and rescue was called off within an hour of its official start that Sunday morning. Lucky was embarrassed more than anything. He called his wife who was ready to kill him for scaring her so badly. He apologized to the park service employees and explained that on two occasions he had asked trail crews to radio out to let someone . . . anyone know that he was alright. I could tell that the park service was disgruntled about not following through with sending someone up to High Bridge the night before to do one last check as they had originally planned to do.

In the end, Ranger Hummel was right; Lucky showed up late but alive. But let's face it, if Lucky had not run into that first trail crew above Milk Creek, he may not ever have found the PCT. At some point he would have run out of food and then what? With no maps and no way to navigate back to a trail he could not find, his prospects would have been bleak at best and fatal at worst. Luck would be on his side though, otherwise this story would have turned out quite differently.

11

Salvation in Skykomish

There are people who go out of their way to help hikers. Sometimes it's a random car ride offered to a grubby hiker by the kindness of a complete stranger. And sometimes it's a person who lives in a town near the trail that lets hikers camp in their backyard or do laundry at their house or grab a shower to wash off days of accumulated dirt and dust. These folks are known in the long-distance hiking world as "trail angels."

The Appalachian Trail and Pacific Crest Trail have a whole host of perennial trail angels – folks that help out hikers year after year. The Continental Divide Trail has just a few but as the CDT gains in popularity, there is sure to be more. Some trail angels are not holed up in one town; they rove and follow the wave of hikers north as they make their way from Georgia to Maine or Mexico to Canada.

One of the better-known trail angel couples on the Pacific Crest Trail is the Saufleys. Jeff and Donna Saufley have been taking in hikers since the mid-90's. Located 454 trail miles north of the Mexican Border, "Hiker Heaven," as they call their backyard, offers a brief respite from the dusty PCT of southern California. The little hamlet of Agua Dulce in which they live does not have much in the way of amenities - no post office and no laundromat. Seeing that there was a void to fill, in addition to a happenstance encounter with a couple of grimy PCT hikers in 1996, the Saufleys found themselves in the role of trail angels before they barely had time to realize what that meant (once word gets out that a couple or family is taking in hikers in a trail town, it's like moths to a flame).

What started as letting a handful of hikers stay in their spare camper one night back in 1996 ballooned to hosting 60+ hikers a night during the high season in 2008. They've since put a 50-person cap on how many hikers they are willing to take in at one time. Even 50 people is too much for their large backyard, in my humble opinion, but not too many for Donna and Jeff. To accommodate this many people, they have gotten really good at crowd control. They've orchestrated an incredibly efficient operation in the form of sign up sheets and help yourself bins full of clean towels, spare clothes to wear while doing laundry and an instruction board that requires little more than knowing how to read. There are sign up sheets for the shower, the computer, and a spare car. That's right. They have a spare car that they allow hikers (read complete strangers) to drive to some of the larger outfitters and gear stops on the far eastern edge of Los Angeles County. And it's all based on trust. And it works. The Saufleys have never had a single thing disappear from their house or their yard during all these years of hosting hikers. How's that for karma?

And the cost . . . well, the cost is whatever each hiker is able to contribute to the mason jar that serves as a donation cup of sorts. Some hikers will kick in $20, $30 and even $50. Others are flat broke and pay nothing. It seems to work out, though. If it didn't, the Saufleys would be just another family in the Agua Dulce phone book and not the best-known trail angels on the PCT.

Not all trail angels offer a laundry list of amenities and services to hikers. Some are in it just for the fun and games. Twenty-four miles north of Jeff and Donna's place lies Casa de

Luna in Green Valley. Casa de Luna is run by the Andersons and the Andersons don't have a spare car for signing out, they don't offer package pick-up or showers or internet. What they do offer is a guaranteed kick-ass time of beer drinking, general hell-raising and taco salad for dinner every night. I've been there twice now and was grateful to get all-you-can-eat taco salad both times, but I just don't know how they eat that dish every night for the entire summer. Don't get me wrong - I love tacos as much as the next guy but after having had them for 47 nights in a row, I'd throw them off a cliff or throw up off a cliff.

Their entry into trail angelhood was also happenstance. Joe Anderson calls it "a serendipitous moment." The way he told it, they ran into a bedraggled-looking couple with backpacks walking around in their town of Green Valley. This couple had gotten off the PCT and come to town to find a restaurant. The male half of this hiking duo desperately wanted some vegetable soup. The only restaurant in town was closed and he was feeling a bit blue as a result. There's nothing more mentally devastating to a long-distance hiker than thinking about food all day and heading into town only to find the only restaurant that serves food closed.

Earlier that day, Joe decided on a whim to make a big pot of vegetable soup. No particular reason really. As a matter of fact, soup is one of the last things Joe typically prepares, a once in a blue moon kind of thing. In one of those completely coincidental instances, Joe and Terri struck up a conversation with this couple that they randomly ran into in town. "Forager" explained how he'd had a hankering for vegetable soup all day and was so disappointed that the restaurant was closed. Joe's eyes lit up like Christmas lights and he invited them to come to their house for dinner.

Ten years later it's not uncommon for them to host as many as 20-30 hikers per night during the high season. Some pass by the Andersons without stopping, after feeling guilty about having spent far too many nights at the Saufleys. It's a shame because staying with the Andersons is one of the highlights of a PCT thru-hike.

Keep in mind that trail angels are few and far between on long trails. It's purely coincidental that the Saufleys and the Andersons are in such close proximity to one another. After heading out of the Andersons, there's not much in the way of trail angels for the next 650+ miles unless you count Hiker Town.

Hiker Town is like stepping into an alternate reality. It exists as a little wayside series of buildings on the edge of Highway 138 somewhere on the western edge of the Mojave Desert. The trail passes within a few feet of the buildings that comprise Hiker Town. I had never even heard of the place when I stumbled upon it back in 2004. The next 24 hours were an odd mix of getting a lift in a Rolls Royce to a convenience store, watching fellow hikers parade around the property on miscellaneous horses, being offered a shower only to find that the water was a degree above freezing, surfing the web in a dilapidated trailer that looked as though it would blow away with the tumbleweeds during the next gust of wind, listening to the howling drunkenness of one of the "caretakers" who was five times as filthy as any hiker staying there and discovering that Jack Fair, the previous owner of the place, had shot and killed himself right there in the main house.

I left Hiker Town wondering what type of crazy time warp I had just walked into. And that was after being awakened by a curious horse at 4:00 A.M. that put his muzzle about 12 inches from my face and snorted.

The current owner is a bit eccentric but not foul-mouthed and prone to fits of rage as the previous owner, Jack Fair, apparently was. Jack allowed PCT hikers to come onto the property and even stay the night but more than one PCT hiker left upset or angry at Jack for something he had said or done. One hiker, "Troubador," recounted his brief stay at Hiker Town back in 1999 when it was simply known as "Jack Fair's Place":

The trail met highway 138. We crossed and walked up Jack Fair's driveway towards his house. The guidebook described Jack Fair as "A concerned citizen who has generously offered water and camping to all through travelers on the PCT."

As we approached the house a shirtless, gray bearded Jack Fair, probably in his late 60's or early 70's emerged along with "Yosemite John." Pointing at Yosemite John (YJ, as he was called for short) Jack asked, "Are all PCT hikers retarded or is it just him?" In unison "Rerun" and I responded, "It's just him."

Jack greeted us. He shook my hand and instantly I smelled like the cigarettes he chain-smoked. He led us to the garage to stow our gear and then invited us into the house. Jack said we could sit anywhere we liked except on the Lazyboy recliner that was dingy, dank and surrounded by cigarette ashes. He lead us into the kitchen and offered me a coke while Rerun stuck with his water.

This is the point in time when Rerun and I stepped off of the PCT and into a wind tunnel of profanity.

Jack Fair was a former motorcycle rider. He drove his motorcycle almost everywhere in North America and now describes himself as a philosopher. As I looked through his trail register, he dropped some articles and papers in *front of us which he asked us to read. Rerun skimmed them slightly while I stuck to the register. Jack said, "Okay, @^#$*$& read them, or don't %#&$*%^# read them. What the %#^@&$^ do I care. You have to live your own @^#%$ life . . . I'm talking to my #&$%#% self now. So if you #&$^#%@ interrupt me, you'll be *^^#%#*%%#* interrupting a private *&%#$@#* conversation."*

After a pause he explained his rates for the use of his house and facilities. "For $1 I'll drive you down the road to the store. For $5 you can camp in the garage and take a shower and I provide the towel. If you just want to hang around for a little bit then it will be $5." Rerun and I looked at one another as if we had been scammed.

We asked Jack for the $1 ride to the store and got into the back of his car. His dog rode up front with him. As I moved to get into the car I glanced at the seat and found it covered in all manner of dirt and grime. Rerun and I looked at each other. Rerun said, "Don't ask."

As we drove down to the store I inquired about the fare. I wanted to be certain of the rate since we had just been duped. "Jack, is it $1 round trip to the store, or $1 each way?" I asked, feeling it was a legitimate question. There was a pause as Jack looked at me in the rearview mirror and said, "Are you some sort of &#^$%@^ @&#^%@^%?" I took that to mean $1 round trip as Rerun laughed hysterically.

Still shaken from the verbal dressing down, I entered the store and made my selections. Rerun did the same and

Jack waited outside. I felt pressure to get and pay for my stuff quickly. I hurried to the car and we were on our way back.

Jack was yelling and cussing up front. The noise of the car with all the windows down kept us from really hearing what he was saying. We both nodded and agreed nonetheless.

Since Rerun and I had been duped out of $5 for just hanging out, we decided to stay for a while and retreated to the garage with our store purchases.

Jack came from the house to the garage in a huff. He yelled, "Okay who was the last #%@&@% @@^#%@^ to use the sink in the house to take a shave?" It was obvious it was neither Rerun or myself as we both had beards. "Perhaps it was YJ?", Rerun offered. "Well, whoever the #&$%$%#& it was pushed the @&@^#@& stopper down on the #^@@#%#% drain and now I can't get it #&%$@&#*$^ open," Jack screamed. His eyes looked away for a moment and his level of rage jumped up 5 notches.

"WHO THE #%$* OPENED THAT @#$&&#^$% DOOR!?!?!?!?" he yelled at the top of his lungs throwing his hands in the direction of a door behind Rerun. "THAT DOOR HASN'T BEEN OPENED IN 10 #^$%@%#$@& YEARS! ANY IDIOT KNOWS THAT IF YOU WANT A #$@^#%#$& CROSS BREEZE YOU GOTTA OPEN THIS #^$%%@%# DOOR!"

Jack slammed one door shut, and then opened the other. Rerun deflated the situation somewhat by offering to look at the sink. Tradja, Neil, Wahoo and YJ walked in as Jack and Rerun were about to depart to the house. I could see the rage forming in Jack as he was preparing to unleash it on YJ. "Did you take a shave in the house?" Jack jabbed at YJ. "Uh, no Jack, I've got three days beard on my face. I was planning on taking a shave, but I haven't gotten to it yet," replied YJ in a half laughing tone. "Well, it's too #%##&& late, I've already blamed you for breaking the #^$%&3% sink," Jack said as he swung into full profanity to explain the situation with the sink again.

At this point I was ready get out of there. Rerun returned from fixing the sink and Jack paid him with two power bars for his services. We then handed Jack the $10 for sitting in his garage for two hours and got some water from the sprinkler.

I would have been really angry about the money Jack charged and the way he went about it, but Smokey had come into Jack's with only a Discover credit card. And when the store - despite having a large Discover sign in their window - declined to accept it, Jack, to his credit, covered the charge.

***

The Appalachian Trail has its trail angels too. Bob Peoples was so enamored with the long-distance hikers that would pass by his place in Tennessee that he built a huge log cabin bunkhouse to accommodate them. Donation based pricing once again. Hikers are offered a daily shuttle down to Newport, Tennessee

. . . the closest town to his Kincora Hiker Hostel. Additionally there are showers, laundry and kitchen facilities. Not bad for a $4 suggested donation per night.

"Dizzy B" was a gruff but nice lady who lived near the AT trail town of Glencliff, New Hampshire. She would drive out Atwell Hill Road every evening during the summer to an abandoned Park Service building known as the "Atwell Hilton." If any hikers were tenting on the lawn, she'd back the truck in and unload firewood. She'd also pull out two coolers: one full of beer and one full of soda. If you want to win over the hearts of long-distance hikers . . . offer them beer and soda. She'd build a fire and chat for a couple of hours with everyone and then take off only to repeat the sequence later the next day and the day after that. The Atwell Hilton has long since been torn down and Dizzy B has moved on, but it was sure nice to get a couple of ice-cold sodas from her in 1999 when I was hiking through.

I once popped out on Pennsylvania Highway 33 at a place called Wind Gap during my AT thru-hike to check my map for directions. At that same exact moment two bicyclists pulled over to check their map for directions. They asked me where I was hiking. I told them to Maine. They gave me that look of disbelief that I'd received many times before when telling folks I was walking from Georgia to Maine. One of the guys pulled out a $20 bill and handed it to me. He told me to go to the bakery in the nearby town of Delaware Water Gap and have some pastries on him. They rode away and I was left there standing with a $20 bill in my hand, dumbfounded that a complete stranger would hand me money for walking. The pastries were fantastic.

In 1999 on the AT, I kept running into this guy who called himself "Desperado." He was a New Jersey State Park Ranger, I believe, and knew all about the thru-hiking community. He even knew who I was without ever having met me. Apparently he would ask hikers he met who was behind them and write down their trail names so he wouldn't forget. He told us that during a typical hiking season, he ended up meeting about half the thru-hikers that came through New Jersey.

The first time I ran into him, he gave me his business card. It simply read "Desperado" in bold font. For occupation it said "Trail Angel." There was a phone number in the bottom corner. The funny thing is that Desperado wasn't operating a business - or at least it didn't appear so. He was handing out slices of pizza on the trail and offering rides to town and info on New Jersey's stretch of the AT. I never needed a ride but some other hikers that got a lift from him told me he had a tape of The Eagles singing *Desperado* that he played continuously while he drove them around. I guess if you were still uncertain that his name was really Desperado after seeing it in bold font on his business card, The Eagles would make sure you knew it was so.

"Meadow Mary" is another well-known roving trail angel on the PCT. I've run into her many times and even got an hour-long ride to a bus station from her back in 2004. She made me change my clothes. Apparently she is quite sensitive to scented detergents. I had just done my laundry and the detergent I used did not agree with her olfactory preferences. She had a spare set of her husband's clothes in her RV luckily for me. I desperately needed a ride to the bus station in Red Bluff, California, in order to get to the Sacramento airport to fly back east for a buddy's wedding. I would have ridden in her camper van naked if it meant getting to that bus station.

The other form of trail angelling that is somewhat common is "the lone cooler." The lone cooler is true trail magic in its purest form; trail magic being what trail angels offer to hikers. A random cooler on the side of the trail full of goodies free for the taking. No fees, no donations, no flat rates and no need to change clothes. Whatever is in the cooler has no strings attached.

Some coolers are chock full of beer, soda, candy bars, chips and cookies and some are empty after getting cleaned out by hikers that had already passed through. You never know what you are going to find until you open the lid. In the case of the cooler we came across in 2008 on the PCT at Santiam Pass in Oregon . . . I'm still not sure what the reddish brown liquid and chunks actually were; however, judging from the shredded wrappers, claw marks and distinct paw prints in the mud beside the lid, my guess is that a bear ate everything in the cooler and then proceeded to barf it all back into the cooler.

I was having a particularly tough day on the AT back in 99' coming out of the Nantahala River in North Carolina. This section of trail had a LOT of ups and downs. "Puds" as some would call them, which is short for "pointless ups and downs." It started with a 3,400' climb and then a bunch of steep descents and more steep ascents. When I reached Stecoah Gap, I was beat and demoralized, not sure if I could move another inch. Just across the road I spied something red in the bushes. Upon further investigation, I realized it was a cooler. I bounded across the highway and whipped open the lid to find freshly made peanut butter and jelly sandwiches and chips and soda. I went from feeling like road kill to a million dollars in the matter of five seconds. I've never been that excited to eat peanut butter and jelly in my entire life.

Feeling reenergized, I was able to make my way to Brown Fork Gap Shelter by dark. Other hikers at the shelter all told me similar stories; they had been beat and tired and the cooler saved their lives! The great thing is that the cooler was left there on the side of the road by a former AT thru-hiker named "Fanny-Pack." Fanny-Pack left a note in the cooler stating that he received a lot of really great trail magic during his 1996 AT thru-hike and wanted to pass the favor forward. It's not un-common for thru-hiker alum to come out and deliver trail magic during subsequent years. This wouldn't be the last Fanny-Pack cooler I came across while on the AT that year. And each time it would be at a crucial spot just after a long climb where I was feeling exhausted. It's as if he knew . . . and he did.

Although the lone coolers were fantastic, the best trail magic that I have ever experienced on a long hike occurred in 2004 in central Washington. It had been raining for weeks and there was no let up in sight. A cold, windy, hypothermic rain. Every day. Rain, rain, rain. I had been hiking in a loose group of half a dozen people and we were all on the same pace to finish at the Canadian Border in late September.

The night before "the greatest trail magic ever," we had all camped near Deep Lake in central Washington's Alpine Lakes Wilderness. We went to bed with rain and woke up to rain and by the looks of the overcast and clouds, we'd be hiking in rain all day. I was a late riser and hiked out of camp last; the bad weather had drained every last ounce of my motivation. A quick perusal of my *PCT Data Book* told me that our campsite was 30.5 miles from Stevens Pass and Highway 2. Highway 2 leads west down to the town of Skykomish and more importantly to the Dinsmores' "Hiker Haven," which was our next town stop.

Following the lead of the Saufleys, Jerry and Andrea Dinsmore started hosting hikers at their abode in 2002. They have a great home on the banks of the Tye River just outside of Skykomish and would pick up hikers at the Pass to bring them down for a stay. We had heard there was a pay phone at the Pass from which you could call them . . . you simply had to get yourself to the Pass.

I didn't want to hike 30.5 miles though. I mean I REALLY didn't want to hike 30.5 miles that day. Actually, I didn't want to get out of my sleeping bag, but I did because that's what hikers do; we get up and hike even if it is cold and wet and miserable. My hope was that the rest of the group didn't want to hike 30.5 miles either. I was mostly going with the flow at this point in the hike and if the entire group hiked all the way to Stevens Pass, I probably would also. But I REALLY didn't want to.

I never caught up to anyone in the group that day. The past few weeks I had been hiking with an umbrella, about which I received heaps of ridicule and mockery. The umbrella was worth its weight in gold, though, and I wouldn't have traded it for anything. It gave me the opportunity to lollygag a bit in the rain. See, most hikers walk very quickly in the pouring cold rain to generate heat and stay warm. Granted, most waterproof jackets keep the rain from seeping in but the cold rain zaps the heat from your upper body through convection. It's just a simple fact of allowing cold water to land on your chest and shoulders for hours on end. With the umbrella, the rain never hits your chest and shoulders and subsequently allows you to stay warmer; it is like walking with a small tent over your head all day. The other thing that hikers wearing only rain jackets typically don't do is they don't take breaks. Who wants to take a break in the pouring rain on the side of the trail only to get more soaked and more cold? I took breaks every hour or so with the umbrella. I could squeeze in and get my entire body under the umbrella's perimeter. It was great, but the more breaks I took and the more I lollygagged, the further behind the crew I got.

At the Surprise Lake Trail junction there was a note in a plastic bag on the middle of the trail. My heart sank. I knew this note was going to be from someone in the group saying they had decided to push all the way into Stevens Pass because of the weather. We had gotten in the habit of leaving notes for one another when the group got split up so I knew it was from one of my people.

I hesitantly walked up to the note, bent over in the heavy rain and picked up the plastic bag. The note read:

Hikers, Tremor and I are taking the Surprise Lake Trail down to Highway 2. It's a shortcut. We are going into Skykomish to get a room tonight come hell or high water. Hope to see you all there. —Trainwreck

Ugh. No! I simply couldn't allow myself to take the Surprise Lake Trail and leave the PCT either. I had set a goal when I started my PCT thru-hike at the Mexican Border that I would hike every inch of the PCT if possible. Taking the Surprise Lake Trail down to the highway would mean leaving the PCT and skipping a 13-mile stretch of the trail. I looked at my watch and it was four-thirty. It would be dark by eight and if I was going into Skykomish today, I'd be hiking in the dark on the PCT to Stevens Pass. I had 13 miles to go. After a quick snack, I embraced my fate and hiked into the pouring rain.

I had originally planned to camp with everybody that night at Josephine Lake, which lay five miles south of the Pass. We would get up early the next morning, hike to Highway 2 and be in Skykomish for breakfast. Or at least that had been the plan this morning. Now the prospects of my camping at Josephine Lake solo in the rain were quite real. I thought that perhaps two of the other hikers in our group, "Jupiter" and "Shep," would still go to Josephine Lake and camp. If they were camped there, I'd definitely stop and camp there.

I arrived at Josephine Lake around dusk. It was bleak, didn't have much in the way of trees for protection from the weather, and Jupiter and Shep were nowhere to be found. I looked at my watch, which told me it was just after seven o'clock. I scarfed down two candy bars while scrounging around for my flashlight. My fate was most definitely sealed. I was hiking into Stevens Pass tonight. As I left the lake behind me, it began pouring again. This was going to be swell.

So here I was hiking at night in the pouring rain with a little keychain flashlight to illuminate my way. Pretty dumb really. If I tripped and fell or slipped and broke an ankle, I'd be in a hypothermic and dangerous situation within minutes. Everyone would assume that I had camped for the night and no one was with me to know otherwise. I had already walked 26 miles (a marathon) and was a bit worn out. Realizing there was no room for error, I focused on every single step and I slowed down a bit. Rushing down the trail in the pouring rain in pitch dark would get me nowhere but hurt.

I remember smiling and laughing a bit as I made my way down to Stevens Pass with umbrella in hand in the middle of a tempest that night. I think I was likely in an exhaustion-induced delirium and would have had my sanity questioned if anyone had happened upon me out there. But there was no one out there . . . why would there be?

The trail spit me out into a dirt parking lot. It was the trailhead parking lot at Stevens Pass and there were no cars there. Anyone who had any kind of sense was at home under a dry roof and not out here in this monsoon. I could see the dimly lit highway just ahead and an 18-wheeler pulled over on the road shoulder. I vaguely remembered someone saying that there was a pay phone at the Pass from which you could call the Dinsmores and they would come pick you up. That payphone wasn't in the trailhead parking lot so I guessed it might be down at Stevens Pass Ski Area, which was about ¼-mile down the road to the west.

I walked down to the ski area to find a series of buildings that were well lit but no one was milling about which made sense given that the ski area didn't open until November and it was September. I thought that maybe, just maybe, there would be an unlocked door and I could steal the night away in a dry janitor's closet or bathroom floor. I spent the next hour walking around the base area and must have pulled on a hundred door handles. The entire place was locked up tight. It was almost ten o'clock and I had to figure out something. The thought of setting up my tent was just too depressing to consider at this point. Maybe the driver of the 18-wheeler had a cell phone?

I walked back up to the Pass as the downpour strengthened. My only chance was to go knock on the door of the idling big rig and hope that I didn't scare the shit out of the driver. I simply had no other options. I started for the truck and noticed a dimly lit streetlamp on the other side of the highway. I followed the lamp down its supporting post with my eyes. It illuminated a metal box. A telephone booth! I was elated but felt like a big idiot having just walked around the ski area for an hour when all along the phone had been on the other side of the highway.

I ran across the empty highway and dodged into the phone booth. The roof was solid and at least I could make this call and figure out what to do out of the rain. The Dinsmores had posted a business card inside the phone booth – what luck! Occupation: Trail Angels. Phone number on the right hand corner. Maybe all these trail angels were using the same business card service? I looked at my watch. It was 10:15 on a Monday night. I paused. Should I really be calling these folks this late on a Monday night? What if they were asleep? What if I pissed them off by calling so late? How could I possibly ask them to come pick me up given the weather and the time of night? I stared out the dirty glass of the phone booth into the rain and contemplated my predicament for a moment. There was nowhere decent to camp and I'd be setting up a wet tent – wet from the previous couple days of rain. Grim at best. It was time to roll the dice.

"Hello."

"Um hello. Is this Jerry?" I asked politely.

"Yep, this is Jerry."

"Hi, this is Disco. I think some of my hiking partners may have come down to Skykomish earlier today," I offered, dancing around the fact that I desperately needed Jerry to come get me. I guess I didn't want to seem that desperate just yet.

"Oh yeah. They were expecting a Disco to call. I picked them up a few hours ago. Let's see, I've got Jupiter, Shep, and GT."

"Oh that's great. I figured they were there," I said trying to figure out how I would go about asking Jerry for a ride.

"Where are you at?" Jerry asked me.

"I'm up here at the Pass. I hate to ask you this late at night but it's pouring up here and I could really use a ride down to town," I offered in a pathetic tone.

"No problem, I'll be right there," Jerry declared without hesitation and that was it.

Twenty minutes later, Jerry pulled up in his big truck and I suggested I get in the back since I was so wet and dirty. He told me not to think of it and to get into the front seat. He had the heat cranked up and I spent the better part of the ride down thanking him profusely for saving me from a miserable night in the cold rain.

I arrived at Jerry's house to find all my friends in dry clothes, freshly showered watching the weather channel. Forecast was for more rain and snow levels coming down to 5,000' - essentially that would mean most of the PCT heading north into Glacier Peak Wilderness, which was our next stretch of trail.

I walked into the kitchen after having left my sopping wet pack and rain jacket at the door. There was a plate of food on the kitchen table and Andrea Dinsmore was smiling at me.

"Eat up," she said with a big grin.

I was floored. I sat down and started in without hesitation. After 30 miles of tramping around all day in the pouring rain, I could have eaten a horse the size of an elephant. I may have eaten seconds and thirds . . . I can't really remember . . . the next ten minutes was a flurry of talking to Andrea, Jupiter, Shep and GT in between mouthfuls of food. They told me the other half of our crew was at a motel in town.

"There's a hot tub upstairs if you want to soak," Jerry said, as if almost forgetting he had one.

My eyes practically popped out of my head. I finished my plate and thanked Andrea a few million more times. I grabbed an extra towel off the bathroom shelf and headed up the stairway to the second story deck. A light drizzle greeted me as I tiptoed onto slick wet wood. I turned off the hot tub lights and hopped into the 104-degree water. I slid in and let out a big long sigh of relief. I stared up at the night sky and could see a break in the clouds off in the distance. Only one short hour ago I was standing inside a phone booth in the middle of nowhere, soaking wet from having walked thirty miles through the rain. Now I sat in the warm waters of the Dinsmores' hot tub with a full belly admiring the irony of it all. It is truly amazing how our fates can change at a moment's notice.

12

Death by Bloodletting

During the summer of 1996, I took a weeklong road trip with my buddy Bill. We were coming off the heels of the road trip of all road trips from the previous summer – a 3,300-mile odyssey from South Carolina to North Dakota and back to visit an old high school chum. That trip ended in a cracked head gasket on a borrowed Ford Tempo and we finished the final leg from Wisconsin to South Carolina on a Greyhound Bus. We were hoping to recreate another great excursion in 1996 – minus the cracked head gasket and bus ride.

So this time around, Bill and I planned a shorter trip . . . just a big loop from South Carolina to the Outer Banks of North Carolina, into Virginia and back home. No one had bothered to mention that the Outer Banks in June have mosquitoes that will cart you away and we never bothered to ask. We found out quite clearly though within a matter of minutes after pulling up at one of the National Park Service campgrounds on Cape Hatteras. Within five seconds of getting out of Bill's car to set up camp, we were assaulted viciously by hordes of mosquitoes. We bid a hasty retreat to Bill's car, jumped in, and locked the doors just to make sure they couldn't get us. We looked at each other blankly and tried to figure out if it was actually possible to experience death by bloodletting.

Until 2008 the mosquitoes on Cape Hatteras were the worst I'd ever experienced. That would all change once we stepped foot into Sky Lakes Wilderness in southern Oregon during my second thru-hike of the PCT. The Oregon snowpack during the previous winter had been well above average, which left lingering snow in the high country that summer. P.O.D. and I had been on a faster pace than I had in 2004 on the PCT and we ended up being in Sky Lakes Wilderness about 3 weeks earlier which was theoretically about six weeks earlier considering the timeframe of the snow melt. Long story short, we showed up during the peak of the mosquito season. The mosquitoes in Sky Lakes made those in Cape Hatteras look like lazy houseflies. It was beyond brutal. We were lucky to escape without requiring a transfusion.

It started innocently enough . . . we had hiked from Ashland, Oregon, to Fish Lake Resort along the Pacific Crest Trail in the July summer heat. Not much in the way of bugs, though. Fish Lake Resort was one of many "resorts" along the PCT in Oregon. It contained a restaurant, small gift shop and some outside picnic tables. It was about a mile off the trail so we hitched down in hopes of finding the restaurant open. It was and we feasted. There is nothing quite like holding a menu in your hands, gazing at all the possibilities after a week's worth of ramen noodles and energy bars.

We stuffed our faces and then ambled down to Fish Lake for a swim. The water was cool and refreshing. I barely wanted to leave but alas, leaving is a constant on long hikes and it was time to log some miles before it got too dark.

We got a quick ride back to the trail with a nice lady who was on her way to Klamath Falls. She dropped us off where we had been standing with our thumbs out just a few hours before. Our goal was another six or so miles before stopping to set up camp for the evening.

The hike up the side of Mt. McLoughlin had an easy gentle grade, which was nice considering the fullness of my belly from wolfing down way too many french fries back at Fish Lake. About an hour in, I noticed a mosquito or two buzzing around. I swatted every now and then without giving too much thought to the pesky little beasts.

Thirty minutes later the intensity picked up and I grabbed my headnet and put it on. P.O.D. was still holding out, saying that they weren't really bothering her. Over the next fifteen minutes the onslaught began in earnest. P.O.D. put her headnet on and we quickened our pace. It must be a natural human instinct to try and outrun things that drive you mad. Hiking faster did little to make our situation any better. It only made us sweat more and breathe harder which actually attracts mosquitoes, as it turns out.

By the time we topped the hill we'd been climbing on our hike out of Fish Lake, we were practically at a full run. I had buried my "all natural" bug repellent deep in my backpack earlier in the day with no possible idea that I would desperately need it just a few hours later. If I chose to stop and dig it out of my pack, it would mean certain bloodletting. No thanks. We found that if we hiked fast enough and swatted frequently enough, it kept the bulk of the bastards at bay.

"What should we do?" I asked with a hint of desperation in my voice.

"We should find the first flat camping area, set up the tent and get in as quickly as possible," P.O.D. replied without hesitation.

Within a couple of minutes of topping the hill we found our flat spot and set up our tent in about 60 seconds flat. I threw my stuff inside, got in and then P.O.D. did the same. We zipped up the tent in a fury and killed the 10 or so little bloodsuckers that got in during our entry. We didn't make our six miles, which was a disappointment, but that was the least of our worries. The real issue was right outside our tent and trying to figure out what we were going to do about it preoccupied our minds for the rest of the night.

"Holy shit," I declared rather bluntly. "That was insane! What the hell are we going to do between here and Crater Lake? It's another 50 miles!"

"I don't know," P.O.D. replied in a defeated voice.

There aren't many obstacles that can't be overcome on a long trail without a bit of persistence and determination. However, I was seriously intimidated by the high-pitched whine of what sounded like a couple million mosquitoes at our tent door. And the thought of miserably enduring a solid 50 miles of those things until we got to Crater Lake where we could buy some real bug spray was demoralizing.

I've had a few run-ins with mosquitoes before and my previous experience told me that at some point during a typical buggy night, it gets cold enough for them to burrow into the ground for warmth and disappear for a while. On this night, that never happened and when I awoke sometime around 3:00 A.M., all I could hear was that same high pitched whine. Bzzzzzzzzzz. At 6:00 A.M. we were fully awake, staring out the mesh of the tent door where the mass of mosquitoes were just waiting for their morning breakfast to come outside.

A strategy session ensued; we needed a plan. Experts will tell you that in any survival situation the first thing you need to do is to take inventory of what gear you have. Although this wasn't really a survival situation in the truest sense of the term, our mental stability hinged on figuring out a way to make the next 50 miles tolerable. The odds were against us considering our lack of DEET and my lack of long pants.

One option, of course, would be to return to Fish Lake Resort or hitch out to the nearest town to buy some legitimate bug repellant and some more gear. And even though we were only five miles from the highway into Fish Lake, the thought of turning back was even more defeating than the thought of going forward into the swarms. It's part of the thru-hiker mindset to constantly move forward. You spend months on end heading in one direction towards one goal and to have to turn around and walk in the opposite direction is simply unfathomable.

Our basic strategy came down to minimizing the time spent not moving while outside the tent. This presented specific problems when using the bathroom. Going #1 is not as big a deal as #2 when being attacked by 200 blood-craving mosquitoes. To deal with this we pre-tore all our toilet paper inside the tent each morning into folded squares. Our "all natural" DEET-free insect repellent was kept easily accessible on our persons - mine in a side shorts pocket and P.O.D.'s in her skirt pocket. I was really envious of her skirt, by the way. It was a long skirt with side snaps that could be worn as a shorter skirt and I had seen more than one dude hiking in them. All I had was the pair of shorts I had been wearing for the last three months and a knee-length homemade rain skirt, each laughable as bug protection and mostly laughable anyway. We both had head-nets, though, and over the course of the week they would be worth their weight in gold, as would our raingear and our MP3 players.

We burst out of the tent that morning and immediately doused ourselves with lemon eucalyptus bug dope. The mosquitoes would still land on me but fly away after deciding that lemon eucalyptus wasn't part of their preferred diet. We packed up with gusto and hiked out with the nervous angst of someone about to miss the bus to work.

I quickly determined that I needed to reapply bug dope every hour to my legs in order to keep them from sucking my blood. That's what I got for trying to be a hippie using all-natural bug dope instead of one containing DEET. Bug repellents containing DEET have been proven to work quite well at warding off mosquitoes. It was originally tested as a pesticide on farm fields & comes with a host of health warnings that have made some people reluctant to use it. I would have gladly bathed in the stuff if someone had presented me with a bottle that morning.

At our first rest break I whipped out my rain jacket and rain skirt and put them on hastily. I then broke open the wrapper on my energy bar and slyly slipped it through a small gap in the bottom of my headnet to take a bite. P.O.D. was having a better time of it due to the skirt she was wearing but she, too, got her rain jacket out and ate her snack through the bottom of her headnet. Within 30 seconds of sitting down, we literally had well over a hundred mosquitoes trying to find any possible way to bare skin on our bodies. All I could think about was some factoid I had read stating that says mosquitoes can sense carbon dioxide from a human 150 feet away. So outside of holding my breath for the next week, there was no escape for me or P.O.D. or anyone else in Sky Lakes Wilderness.

As we were sitting there on the ground in the swarms, pretending to enjoy our snack break, a big guy in black shorts and a black t-shirt came ambling up the trail. He had no headnet, no hiking pants and definitely no rain skirt. He looked miserable.

"How's it going?" I asked him.

"These bugs are terrible," he replied getting straight to the point.

"Do you have a headnet or any pants?" I asked gingerly.

"Nope. Got a big can of bug spray though." He pulled out a large metal can of aerosol bug spray that instantly made both P.O.D. and I extremely jealous.

"I'm hiking all of Oregon to lose weight. Started a week ago down in Ashland," Mike told us as he swatted at the mosquitoes that didn't seem to be that affected by his big can of bug spray.

We headed out of our break spot after more than a few mosquitoes had figured out they could sneak through the openings in the bottom of our headnets. I glanced back and saw Mike still standing at our break spot swatting incessantly. Poor bastard.

As day one faded into day two, we honed our strategy a bit . . . especially with going #2. I found that pre-digging a hole in the ground and then backing off and running around confused the mosquitoes. I would set my pre-torn toilet paper beside the hole and then run around some more. The mosquitoes were having trouble figuring out what I was doing, which is exactly what I wanted.

At the last possible second before soiling my shorts, I would pull them down and hit both cheeks with a spray of lemon eucalyptus repellant. Squat, release, wipe, cover hole, throw backpack on and then speed away all in less that 60 seconds. Unbelievably efficient and extraordinarily ridiculous. I should probably patent this technique.

That night, after scrambling to the protection of our fully enclosed tent, we realized that the 16 oz. plastic tub of almond butter we brought from Ashland just might serve double duty in our current situation. During our initial desperate inventory of gear, we hadn't considered this plastic tub for anything other than holding almond butter.

"We could use this tub as a piss cup," P.O.D. stated with the enlightenment of a Buddhist monk.

"Huh?" I offered up not quite understanding how this would work for her.

"Yes, that's it. We can use it to pee into so that we won't have to get out of the tent at night or in the morning," she proclaimed.

"How the heck are you going to squat over this tub and get your aim right considering the four inch diameter?" I asked not believing her.

"There's only one way to find out," she said with a grin on her face.

That night in the tent I found out that a woman can pee in a cup with the same accuracy that any man can. I also found out that sometimes I have more urine in my bladder than a 16 oz. cup will hold! Not fun but the tradeoff of keeping my blood supply intact was well worth it.

By day three we were well over halfway between Fish Lake and Crater Lake National Park and I was getting pretty good at dealing with the ever present mosquito hordes. I learned that by wearing my rain jacket with hood up and mosquito headnet on, rain skirt in place, lemon eucalyptus slathered from knees down and headphones in my ears, I could transport myself to another dimension mentally and remain mostly untouched by the mosquitoes. This strategy worked well until my MP3 player died.

The one remaining problem I couldn't solve was peeing during the day. In normal hiking mode, I'd walk along and pull over to the side of the trail to take a leak. These mosquitoes were anything but normal and we were not in normal hiking mode given the current mosquito pandemic going on in Sky Lakes Wilderness. As soon as I stopped and exposed myself, I got swarmed. Getting bitten by a mosquito on the most private of privates is something I wouldn't wish on my worst enemy. I found that if I swayed around like a boat on the high seas while peeing it would keep the mosquitoes confused but every now and again one would still kamikaze its way in and hit the bull's-eye.

I needed to step up my game if I was going to keep my sanity. I had read a story about long-distance hiker Andrew Skurka hiking and peeing at the same time for the sake of efficiency during his 6,700-mile Great Western Loop hike. He concluded that stopping to pee took up about 15 minutes a day total while hiking. Over the course of seven months, that would equate to roughly 52 hours or over two full days just of peeing during his hike. I wasn't as concerned about efficiency for the sake of timing like Andy, but I did see value in being able to keep moving while peeing in mosquito country.

My first few attempts resulted in a wet rain skirt and damp shoes. I finally figured out that the way to do the walk-pee sequence successfully was to widen the stance and walk more slowly. With a little practice I got quite good at it. I can only imagine what a passing hiker would have surmised if they had happened by while I was ambling down the trail with junk in hand watering the bushes. That never happened to me, but P.O.D. wasn't so lucky.

P.O.D. had developed her own method of urinating while in mosquito country that would make most women turn red and disown her from the sisterhood.

On her Appalachian Trail thru-hike in 2002, she had perfected urinating while standing upright. And she will brag about this to anyone willing to listen. The process is fairly straightforward she explained. It involves standing with feet at a wide spacing, moving the crotch of her shorts to the side and releasing. It's true guys . . . women can pee standing up. If you don't believe me, spend a week on any of the Big Three (AT, PCT, CDT) long trails during the summer months and hike around women . . . invariably you will find out.

P.O.D. determined that she had to tweak her standing-while-peeing technique in Sky Lakes Wilderness if she was going to survive. If she stopped and took too long to actually start peeing, the ever-present mosquitoes would nail her. She wasn't able to walk and pee at the same time like me or even stand and sway. The result ended up in wet shoes. However, she made the process more efficient by holding back to the absolute last second and then with lightning speed, pulling her skirt up with one hand and swatting mosquitoes with the other. She got quite good at this; she also got a bit complacent about looking to see if anyone was around.

We were hiking along the day before we reached Crater Lake and it was getting close to dusk. We had seen only one person in the last four days and had simply assumed that no one in their right minds would be hiking in Sky Lakes Wilderness right now unless they had to. Thru-hikers had to. It's just simply part of the deal when you are trying to walk from the border of one country to the border of another during a short span of time. You've got to keep moving.

P.O.D. was about 30 feet ahead of me and even though it was getting dark and I was wearing a headnet, which decreases vision, I could see that three Forest Service trail crew guys were heading in our direction and were about 100 feet in front of us. Each had on a yellow hard hat and one had a long crosscut saw over his shoulder. I instantly felt sorry for these guys having to do trail work in this mosquito hell and then felt less bad when I considered that they were getting paid. Something that P.O.D. and I were not.

P.O.D. had her head down, headnet on, rain jacket on and MP3 player earbuds in her ears. She was hiking in "oblivion mode." Then she stopped in the middle of the trail, pulled her skirt up with one hand and started swatting with the other. I started laughing instantly as I knew she hadn't bothered to look up to see the trail crew guys walking in our direction only 30 feet in front of her. And she couldn't hear me yell because of her MP3 player.

Being the gracious US Forest Service employees that they were, they immediately turned their heads and stepped off the trail. P.O.D. finished, looked up, turned red and hiked on. I walked by them and said hello with a chuckle. I caught up with P.O.D. and we laughed for a good long while about what had just happened.

If you ever find yourself at a bar in Klamath Falls, White City, or anywhere in southern Oregon for that matter and overhear a Forest Service employee telling tale of a six foot tall woman who can pee while standing up, it just might be my fiancée he is talking about.

~ Epilogue ~

P.O.D. and I made it through mosquito hell in one piece and finished our thru-hike of the PCT. Realizing that I had found someone who shared my affinity for long trails and even longer hikes, I wised up and asked her to marry me the following summer. For some odd reason she said yes.

Shortly thereafter we left the town of Crested Butte, Colorado, which we had called home for the previous four years, and moved to Denver. As much as we would have liked to stay in Colorado's "Last Great Ski Town," we needed to move to the city to pursue some long-term goals.

I found a job as a full-time forester and P.O.D. landed a teaching position while pursuing a graduate degree on the side. Suffice it to say that things have changed a bit since we last walked 2,663 miles on the PCT in 2008. One thing that hasn't changed is our passion for the outdoors and hitting the trail.

Our hikes now end up being much shorter than five months. We completed a 90-mile section of the CDT in Colorado's Weminuche Wilderness last summer that blew are minds. We've hit the trails in both Maui and Kauai over the last two winters. This summer we are branching out a bit and plan to do our first stint of international hiking: a couple of weeks of Spain's GR11 in the high Pyrenees.

It's not quite the same, though. Five months on a trail is a chance of a lifetime. Four of those five-month trips will ruin you for life! There is true freedom on the trail. You answer to no one. There is no morning commute or climbing of the corporate ladder. There is no clock-punching or working your way into middle management. There is no multi-tasking. There is only the trail and the singular goal of reaching some distant border or ending point many months down the road. It's quite beautiful in its simplicity.

People you meet on a long hike become fast friends in a way that takes six months back here in the civilian world. I'm lucky to live in an area with a sizeable hiking contingent; Denver and Boulder probably have one of the largest groups of thru-hiker alumni in the US. I bowl with folks I hunkered down with in pouring rainstorms on the PCT in 2004. I hoist beers with hikers who trudged through Montana on the CDT with me in 2006. And best of all, I share a house and a life with a hiker I have hiked 5,000 miles with! I might not be on the trail at the moment, but I've got the next best thing.

A famous long-distance hiker named "Roni from Israel" once said, "I'm addicted to hiking. It's a disease. There are people that drink alcohol everyday, people who smoke . . . I Hike! Or theoretically hike when I'm able to get up in the morning." Me too, Roni. I just put a "Gone Hiking" sign on my office door. My backpack is loaded; it's time to hit the trail.

~ Acknowledgements ~

There are so many people that I owe a debt of gratitude to in the making of this book. I'd like to thank the initial reviewers of the early drafts: Kiki and Gary Dotzler, Don and Gretchen Bunnel, Scott Stewart, Matti Urlass, Matthew Jackson, Linda Patton, Scott Herriott, Tim Hogeboom, Glen Van Peski, Jamie Carroll, Mike Keith and my parents.

I'd like to thank the following folks for providing blurbs for the book: Justin Lichter, Philip Werner, Paul Magnanti, Tim Hogeboom, Geolyn Carvin, Teresa Black and Glen Van Peski.

A special thanks goes to Rebecca Taylor for scouring the book with a legal eye and providing me continuous feedback during the final stages of the book's production. Thanks goes to Aaron Wykhuis for reviewing the final draft.

Additionally I'd like to thank my friend and fellow hiker Brian Clark for letting P.O.D. and I occupy his guest bedroom for a month when we initially moved to Denver. His "yoga room" provided an amazing space to write this book.

I'd like to thank Arvin Ram of Townie Books in Crested Butte and Glen Van Peski for providing me with motivation at crucial times to follow through with the production of this book. It's easy to let self-doubt get in the way of higher ambitions and both of them helped me keep plugging away.

A big thanks to the folks at Gossamer Gear including Grant Sible. His can-do demeanor and passion for the long-distance hiking community is why I love being a Gossamer Gear Trail Ambassador.

Thanks goes to Richard Larson for allowing me to use that amazing photo for the cover of this book. Luckily for me, I was in the right place at the right time when he had his camera in hand.

A special debt of gratitude goes to Scott Herriott. He answered my countless questions during the editing of my film *The Walkumentary* and wrote the Foreword for this book without that much of a fight.

And to my family I owe special thanks. My sister Nell believed in me throughout this entire process and for that I can't thank her enough. And I can't wait to read her first novel! My dad's response after reading the first draft of this book was, "Well son, it looks like you've got yourself a book." That comment and the continued encouragement he has provided me throughout my life has helped me see that anything truly is possible with a little bit of motivation and a dose of ambition. And to my mom, a retired elementary school librarian and corrector of bad grammar my entire life, I simply can't thank her enough for being my editor on this book. Her insight and mastery of English grammar kept this book out of the gutter (almost).

To my wife and best friend, Felicia, I owe the world and a vase of flowers. You put up with me during this whole process and once again our relationship is still intact (I think). Your companionship on 5,000+ miles of hiking is something I value more than I'll ever be able to put into words.

And finally, to the trails and the great people that hike them, this book would not have been possible without the company of both.

~ About the Author ~

Lawton Grinter is an author, documentary filmmaker, forester, trail runner and veteran long-distance hiker having completed end-to-end hikes of the Appalachian Trail, Continental Divide Trail and two hikes of the Pacific Crest Trail. In addition to the "Big 3″ he has also hiked the John Muir Trail and Colorado Trail in his 10,000+ miles of long-distance hiking since 1999. He filmed, edited and produced the trail documentary entitled "The Walkumentary" which covered his 2006 southbound Continental Divide Trail hike. He currently lives in Denver, Colorado with his wife and fellow long-distance hiker Felicia Hermosillo and their dog Gimpy. This is his first book.

CPSIA information can be obtained at www.ICGtesting.com
Printed in the USA
LVOW08s1801010514

384064LV00003B/322/P